Cecile Macneill Thomson

'Tween the Gloamin' and the Mirk

Poems and Songs

Cecile Macneill Thomson

'Tween the Gloamin' and the Mirk
Poems and Songs

ISBN/EAN: 9783337179588

Printed in Europe, USA, Canada, Australia, Japan

Cover: Foto ©Thomas Meinert / pixelio.de

More available books at **www.hansebooks.com**

'TWEEN THE GLOAMIN' AND THE MIRK.

POEMS AND SONGS.

BY

CECILE MACNEILL THOMSON.

ABERDEEN:
A. KING AND COMPANY.
1882.

TO

MY NATIVE HIGHLANDS,

AND TO

Mrs. Mary MacKellar,

THE HIGHLAND POETESS,

THIS SMALL VOLUME

IS AFFECTIONATELY DEDICATED.

INDEX.

	PAGE
'Tween the Gloamin and the Mirk,	1
Oor Ain Auld Hoose,	2
Sunset on Loch Awe,	4
Farewell,	6
October,	7
Only a Sprig of Snow-white Heather,	8
The Rose of Argyll,	9
Grannie's Bairn,	10
Snowdrops,	12
The Sea Bird,	13
My Maggie, O,	14
Teddy Malone,	15
The Flowers of the 'Teviot,	16
In Memoriam,	17
The Border Land,	18
Haste Thee, O Gentle Spring,	19
Ettrick Jean,	21
Autumn,	22
Seasonable Wishes,	23
Adrift,	24
Garnered Sunbeams,	25
Bonnie Nell,	26
Scotia,	27
Edinburgh,	28
Music and Poesy,	28
The Days of Yore,	29
Lady May,	30
There cam an Auld Man,	32
The Bridge,	32
Grief,	33

Index.

	PAGE
Jeanie,	34
A Silver Wedding,	35
Cradle Song,	36
Bessie,	36
To Majorie,	37
Cladich Burn,	38
Love Long Ago,	39
Experience,	40
My Little One gone,	41
Evening Dreams,	42
Isabel's Lament,	43
My Bonnie Mary,	44
The Storm,	45
A Seance,	46
An Old Maid's Soliloquy,	48
Friendship's Farewell,	49
A Highland Lassie,	51
Latrelle,	52
The Pleasures of Fancy,	53
Ivy,	54
Wealth *versus* Poverty,	55
Lurline,	56
Night,	58
Katie's Secret,	59
Asleep,	60
The Border Lads,	61
Moonlight Memories,	62
Come to the Woodlands,	63
On the River,	64
Isabelle,	65
Roses,	66
Sunless Days,	67
Elwand's Fairy Dean,	68
Birthday Wishes,	69
Always,	70
Dunedin's Welcome,	71
The Winter of the Heart,	72
A Legend,	74
In Memoriam,	75
To Mrs. Mary Mackellar,	76
Mother,	77
A Happy New Year,	77
Ye Minstrel's Tryst,	78

Index.

	PAGE
The Flower of Glensheira,	80
My Ring,	82
Uncertainty,	82
My Heart Clings to Thee,	83
My Ain Lad,	84
Friendship,	85
My Wee Wifie,	86
Alone,	87
Our Own,	88
The Cameronian's Dream	89
Awaken,	91
Mary,	92
The Mother and her Boy,	93
The Master is Coming,	96
By Moonlight Alone,	97
Epistle to H.,	98

PART SECOND.

The Pursuit of Light,	101
The Twilight Hour,	108
Live Looking to Jesus,	109
My Refuge,	110
Go Tell thy Griefs to Jesus,	111
In the Valley,	112
Retrospect,	112
Faith, Hope, and Charity,	114
In Memory of Janet,	114
I.H.S.,	116
Yonder,	117
'Mid the Shadows,	118
He giveth his Angels charge o'er thee,	119
Holy Jesus, keep me pure,	120
My Redeemer Liveth,	121
Far Away,	122
The Bible,	124
Home of My Heart,	125
Charity,	126
At the Gates,	128
Rest,	130

Index.

	PAGE
Farewell,	131
Miserere,	132
A Broken Flower,	133
The Mediator,	134
The Good Shepherd,	135
Wearied,	136
Reminiscences of a Communion Sabbath,	137

'TWEEN THE GLOAMIN' AND THE MIRK.

I met thee ere life's early morn
    Had tint its roseate flush ;
I loved thee ere a shade of scorn
    Had tinged thy maiden blush ;
I woo'd thee 'neath the white maythorn,
    Where sang the mottled thrush.

I sought thee when the roses bloomed
    'Neath summer's azure skies ;
My hopes were crushed, life's joy was doomed,
    By those low brief replies ;
False to thyself, 'twas not assumed—
    The love-light in thine eyes.

I had not rowth of glittering gold,
    But a true heart, warm and free
(I will not think that thine was cold) ;
    I would have died for thee :
I loved and lost—the story old—
    For lack of high degree.

And yet, in life's grey gloamin' here,
   I find thee left alone;
The treasures which ye held so dear
   Now scattered are and gone;
The golden hair is getting sere,
   The roseate hues have flown.

But yet to me thou art as fair
   As when, in days of yore,
We breathed the perfumed summer air
   On youth's bejewelled shore;
And now when wintry wastes lie bare,
   I ask thine hand once more.

One little hour with me to watch
   Life's gathering shadows creep;
One lingering ray of light to catch,
   Ere night's dark pinions sweep;
One golden gleam of love to snatch,
   Ere death's oblivious sleep.

OOR AIN AULD HOOSE.

It's weel tae ha'e some siller,
   And there's something in a name,
But the best o' earthly blessings
   Is a guid and happy hame.
It's no in rank nor siller,
   For, whatever be oor lot,

Oor ain Auld House.

Hame aye is hame,
   Be it castle, ha', or cot ;
Sae the Duke may prize his palace,
   And the Laird his manor roose,
But gi'e me the cosy comforts
   O' oor ain Auld Hoose.

Weel theekit is the riggin',
   And weel steekit is the door ;
The fireside is clean,
   And, though carpetless the floor,
It's trim and canty baith,
   And better than its braw,
For hame's aye hame,
   Be it castle, cot, or ha' ;
Sae tae me there's no anither
   That I think sae snug and douce
As the clay-biggit wa's
   O' oor ain Auld Hoose.

The wark has tae be dune,
   But there's willin' hands to work,
And love lichtens labour
   Frae the morning till the murk.
When weary wi' your toilin',
   A' the sweeter comes the rest ;
Often strangers treat ye kindly,
   Yet ane's ain hame is best ;
At least, I ken mysel',
   I'm ne'er sae blythe and croose
As when sittin' by the ingle,
   In oor ain Auld Hoose.

SUNSET ON LOCH AWE.

Fair, lone Loch Awe!—thy soothing breast
Hath hushed the mountain winds to rest;
No vagrant breeze disturbs the calm,
Whilst dewy eve distils her balm
O'er flowery mead and ferny glen;
In nooks beyond the tourist's ken,
The western sky is glowing bright
With garnered remnants of the light,
Refulgent from the setting sun,
Like golden laurels, victor won.
Within the portals of the night
The monarch veils his glorious might,
Yet leaves a scene of splendour rare,
More brilliant than the noontide glare.
The fleecy cloudlets floating slow,
Reflect the gorgeous crimson glow,
Like ruby-tinted opal thrones
Afloat on waves of burnished bronze;
Ethereal balconies that lie
Betwixt the earth and azure sky;
An orchestra for angel choirs,
Where they may tune their golden lyres
In strains celestial; to their king
Sweet vesper hymns they softly sing,
As evening offerings, angel-given,
For earth-stained wanderers seeking heaven.
The slanting sunbeams glance and gleam
From every rill and mountain stream;

Sunset on Loch Awe.

While mirrored in the placid deep
Lies roseate cloud, and wooded steep.
Where sleeps the dead on Innishail
I hear the sea-gull's eerie wail;
In circling flights they may be seen,
The guardians of that island green.
Lone Innishail! I love to stray
Amongst thy ruins, grim and grey,
Where dwelt the holy sister band,
When Romish abbots ruled the land.
Now desolate, the hallowed ground
Gleams like an emerald crystal bound,
Reflecting bright that gilded ray
Which brings the parting kiss of day.
But sunset lends its latest smiles
To Innistrynich's lovely isle,
Where art and nature have designed
A Highland home, by taste refined,
There, sturdy oak, and graceful beech,
There mountain pine, and flowering peach,
In pleasing contrast, proudly wave
By shores which silvery waters lave;
An earthly Eden, fair and mild,
Amid the mountains stern and wild.
On lone Loch Awe, the fading light
Forbodes the creeping shades of night;
Ben Vorich's dark and rugged brow
Is veiled in purpling shadows now.
No longer ruby-tinted cloud,
But gloom and mist, descending, shroud
Those towering peaks which pierce the sky,

Where winter's snows in summer lie.
The gloaming shades to darker eve,
And bats and owls their hidings leave;
The blackbird pipes a mournful lay,
As requiem for departed day.
The twilight deepens into night,
And Luna sheds her silvery light
O'er loch and hill and woodland green,
Till lovelier is the moonlight scene
Than yon fair sunset on Loch Awe,
Which two short hours ago I saw.

FAREWELL.

Farewell, dear boy! The Shepherd needeth thee
    In yon fair fold;
With loving clasp, he leadeth thee
    O'er streets of gold;
Up to the inner court, where sweet-voiced seraphs sing
Unending praises to their glorious King:
    Farewell, dear boy!

Farewell, dear boy! Thou bliss hast early gained,
    We, linger 'mongst the years;
But thou, no sorrow e'er thy young heart pained,
    No burning tears
Hath seared thy life's sweet bloom,
No fairer blossom decks the flower-wreathed tomb:
    Farewell, dear boy!

Farewell, dear boy!   Dost know the grief-cloud lowers
   Beneath the starry dome?
'Bove which, thy dear feet wander 'mid the flowers,
   In thy fair home;
Dost know aught of our sad heart's aching?
To us, the fragrant morn brings no glad waking:
   Farewell, dear boy!

Farewell, dear boy!   Though yet awhile we mourn
   Our darling lost,
We know thou art by angel's gentle care upborne,
   Not tempest tossed;
But safe, thou waitest on the gem-strewn shore,
Thy loved ones coming, there to part no more:
   Farewell, dear boy!*

OCTOBER.

The lang days o' simmer are wearin' awa',
Red-ripe is the rowan, the hip and the haw;
The roses are faded, the lilies are dead,
And awa' owre the ocean the swallows have fled.
Gleefu' the soonds frae the hairst field that's ringin',
Where licht-hearted reapers love ditties are singin';
Sae blithe are the lassies that echo the strains,
And coy are the glances they cast on the swains.

The lang days o' simmer are wearin' awa',
The hichts o' Ben Vorich are silvered wi' snaw;
The saft breeze o' simmer sighs roond us nae mair,
But chill blaws the north wind, and frosty the air.

  * Harold Willouby Lowe.

The woodlands are buskit in yellow and broon,
And sadly the sere leaves are flichtering doon;
The wild bird's sweet warbling is hush'd in the dell,
They have sung their last chorus, to simmer farewell.

The lang days o' simmer are wearin' awa',
The lang nichts o' winter creep eerie owre a';
The mists of October lie white o'er the dale,
And the blue lift abune looks cheerless and pale.
E'en sae comes the autumn o' time to us a',
And sadly and serely oor joys fade away';
Bricht was the spring time, the simmer was gay,
But life, like the seasons, grows chilly and grey.

ONLY A SPRIG OF SNOW-WHITE HEATHER.

'TIS only a sprig of snow-white heather,
    Gathered yestreen from a highland brae—
Blooming unseen through the warm, bright weather,
    But gathered yestreen i' the gloaming grey.
Purple the hills, in their autumn splendour,
    Golden the tints of the woodlands gay;
Far in the distance, softly tender,
    Lingered the smile of departing day.

'Tis only a sprig of snow-white heather,
    Gathered yestreen i' the gloaming grey—
Blooming unseen through the warm, bright weather,
    But gathered yestreen from that highland brae.

Breezes sweet o'er the hillside stealing,
    Stirring the calm of the scented air;
Curtaining shades of the night concealing
    Hill and vale in that landscape fair.

'Tis only a sprig of snow-white heather,
    Gathered yestreen on a highland brae,
Where, hand in hand, we had stood together,
    Watching the gleam of the sun's last ray.
Hand in hand, up life's brae together,
    Go we now, till endeth the day: *
" Tender and true," so meaneth the heather—
    Tender and true, till life's gloaming grey!

THE ROSE OF ARGYLL.

Sweet is this gloaming hour,
Fair is yon dewy flower,
    Bright is the starry gem set in the blue;
But sweeter than gloaming hours,
Fairer than dewy flowers,
    Is the maiden who keepeth her trysting so true.

Under the rowan tree
Gracefully waiteth she;
    I 'mongst the leafy shade hide me awhile;
There softly repeating
Some words of fond greeting
    To welcome my darling the Rose of Argyll.

Wand'reth she slowly,
Head drooping lowly,
   Wond'ring where tarrieth he whom she waits,
Lovingly lingering,
Absently fingering
   The wild rose she plucked from the brier-twined gate.

Forth from my leafy screen,
Still by the maid unseen,
   I clasp to my fond heart my darling so true,
Startling my shy fawn,
To blush like the bright dawn
   That lends to white Jura the rose's red hue.

Under the rowan tree
Over the dewy lea,
   The moonbeams were falling where lingered we twain ;
Sealed with a yielded kiss
Was a low whispered yes,
   Which told that my true heart had not loved in vain.

GRANNIE'S BAIRN.

Big blue een and auburn hair,
Rosy cheeks, and brow sae fair,
Hame-made claes, shoon shod wi' airn—
Such was Mailie, Grannie's bairn.

Grannie's Bairn.

Reared in yon wee theekit hoose,
Grannie's bairn, sae wise and douce,
Early learns wi' Grannie's care,
The airts o' reading, thought, and prayer.

Learns to spell in Grannie's book,
In which, wi' thoughtful, happy look,
Grannie reads frae day to day
How to walk the heavenward way.

Coorin' owre a fire o' peats
Grannie's bairnie sits and greets—
Greets owre thochts when, Grannie gane,
Mailie maun be left alane.

Clasps her hands and breathes a prayer,
That God may lang her Grannie spare.
And when He taks the ane awa,
Just to let Mailie gang and a'.

Sair the pain in Mailie's heart,
When frae Grannie she maun part ;
Bitter tears which nane micht see,
Earnest wishes she could dee.

A' her love in Grannie's grave,
What cares Mailie for the lave ;
Bitter cups she now maun pree
'Mang strangers void o' charitie.

Years hae fled owre Mailie's heid
Sin' her dear auld Grannie deid,
Mony a mile her feet hae trod
Alang life's weary, rugged road.

But still, within her breast concealed,
Loving memories fragrance yield;
And those first impressions bloom
In flowers poetic, tinged with gloom.

SNOWDROPS.

FAIR emblem of Hope, sweet herald of Spring;
Angel-like floweret, what memories ye bring,
Memories of childhood I muse on again,
Scenes from life's landscape o'ershadowed by pain.

Snowdrop, sweet snowdrop, I loved thee of yore;
Bright gem in the mantle thy wintry nurse wore;
Oft have I wandered through woodland and dell
In search of my favourite, thou bonny white bell.

Snowdrop, pure snowdrop, thy blossoms were twined
'Mong the lilies, and roses, and orange combined,
Which wreathed the dark tresses of hazel-eyed May,
When bridal-robed smiled she one sunny Spring day.

Snowdrops, white snowdrops, bedewed with my tears,
Again I recall through the grief-bedimmed years
A death-darkened chamber, where silent and cold
Lay wreathed with the snowdrops the flower of our fold.

Dear emblem of Hope, sweet herald of Spring,
Angel-like floweret, those memories ye bring,
Bright memories of pleasure, sad musings of pain,
Blended to bid thee fond welcome again.

THE SEA-BIRD.

I WOULD that I was a sea-bird wild,
    And my home on the ocean deep,
I'd pillow my head on a sunlit wave,
    Where, rocked by the breeze I'd sleep,
    Where, rocked by the breeze I'd sleep.

Far away from the haunts of men,
    Away o'er the dark blue sea,
I'd wing my flight till the daylight waned,
    Then a billow my couch should be,
    Then a billow my couch should be.

I'd rise on the crest of the snow-tipped wave,
    And bathe in its watery dell,
I'd smooth my plumes with the sparkling spray,
    My mirror a pink-lined shell,
    My mirror a pink-lined shell.

Then away, away, at the rosy dawn,
    To greet the rising sun,
To welcome him back at the gates of light,
    When his triumph o'er night is won,
    When his triumph o'er night is won.

To hail the beams from his golden car,
    When they gild the sea-bird's nest—
To watch the might of his glorious light,
    Till he sinks in the crimson west,
    Till he sinks in the crimson west.

O who would not love the sea-birds wild!
    So beautiful, bright, and free;
And who would not love their ocean home,
    With its beautiful sea-birds—grand old sea—
    Beautiful sea-birds! Beautiful sea!

MY MAGGIE, O.

My Maggie's charming, young, and free,
Gay mirth looks frae her lauchin' ee',
Nae wanton wiles o' art has she,
    But sweetly coy is Maggie, O.

In wavy tresses streams her hair,
Nae raven's wing may it compare,
Devoid o' art's deceiving care,
    In native beauty flowing, O.

Young Maggie is the fairest flower
That decks auld Robin's rosy bower,
What though the lassie hae nae dower,
    Boon gowd or gear, she's priceless, O.

Gin I had but yon rustic cot,
Wi' Maggie as the mistress o't,
Then mine wad be a blissfu' lot,
    The king himsel' micht envy, O.

TEDDY MALONE.

'TWAS late in September, ah, well I remember,
    I parted from Teddy, my heart aching sore;
By yonder lone shieling, controlling my feeling,
    I bade him farewell, to meet him no more.

And Ted, as he kissed me, and fondly caressed me,
    While his dark eyes were misty with sorrowful pain,
Cried good bye, mavourneen, God bless you, and keep you,
    An' soon I'll be back to my colleen again.

My true-hearted Teddy, so faithful and steady,
    Ah, cruel was I to deceive you like this,
I knew that you loved me, your tenderness moved me,
    And sorely, and surely, your presence I'll miss.

But from Scotia's dark mountains, and wild foaming fountains,
    Another is coming to claim me his bride;
The vows they are spoken, which may not be broken
    Through life I have promised to walk by his side.

With gold from his coffers, Black Donald made offers,
    And bought from my father this maiden's sad heart;
Ah, Ted, need you wonder, I'd fain break asunder
    The fetters which force me, from thee, now to part.

But, from love and its beauty, I turn me to duty,
    To shield my poor parents I yield to their choice,
My father is failing, my mother is ailing,
    And urging our bridal, sounds Donald's deep voice.

Then farewell, my Teddy, so faithful and steady,
    It grieves me to think that I'd e'er cause you pain;
Good bye, my darling, God bless you, and keep you,
    For ne'er must I see thee, my own love again.

THE FLOWERS O' THE TEVIOT.

By Teviot's stream, which gently flows
    Through yonder rich romantic dale;
'Mong sheltering scenes, a peerless rose
    Adorns the sweet sequestered vale.
The heath-bell blooms beside the rill,
    The May-flower decks the daisied lea,
But owre them a' on yonder hill,
    The flower o' Teviot bears the gree.

Fair France hath flowerets brightly gay,
    Italia's roses richly bloom,
Dear England wreathes her snowy May
    Wi' Scotia's heath and gowden broom.

I lo'e the hawthorn's dewy spray,
    I lo'e the lilies, sweetly pale,
But let me ha'e to grace my lay,
    The fair white rose o' Teviotdale.

O Borderland! my heart aye warms
    To list thy praises, said or sung,
And none more sweetly sings thy charms,
    Than Teviot's maiden, blithe and young.
Our Border lassies a' are fair,
    O' Scotia's flowers the pick and wale,
But wha amang them can compare
    Wi' yon sweet rose o' Teviotdale.

IN MEMORIAM.

TIBBIE SHIEL, DIED JULY 23, 1878.

ENMANTLED wi' mist are the green hills o' Yarrow,
    In Ettrick the shadows brood dark o'er the vale,
And lonely St. Mary's lies sunless in sorrow,
    As the breeze on its bosom sighs forth its sad tale.

Oh! why wails the wind 'mang the trees o' the forest?
    And why wears sweet summer her vestures of woe?
Fair nature oft smileth when hearts ache the sorest,
    And sunny flowers bloom o'er our dead lying low.

But Yarrow is sad, and her sons they are sighing
    For the death of a mother—the aged and dear;
The dew on the green sward like big tears is lying,
    And husky with grief are the voices we hear.

Long, long, by St. Mary's hath stood her lone dwelling—
　　The haunt of the poets in bright days of yore,
And many have listened their kind hostess telling
　　Her mem'ries of Wilson and rich Border lore.

But now 'neath the green sod in Ettrick she's lying,
　　Where the friends of her childhood have long lain asleep,
And there slumbers Hogg, whom she tended when dying,
　　Together they rest where the shadows lie deep.

THE BORDER LAND.

O Border Land! O Border Land!
　　Ye'll aye be dear to me,
Frae distant isle, and foreign strand,
　　My heart gaes back to thee.

For weel I lo'e thy purpling hills,
　　And wimplin' siller streams;
The music of thy mountain rills
　　Haunts memory's twilight dreams.

I've wandered by thy classic Tweed,
　　And climbed thine Eildons three;
I've roamed owre Ettrick's daisied mead,
　　And Yarrow's flowery lea.

By Gala's banks and Teviot's braes,
　　I've watched the e'enin' fa',
And marked the gowden westlin' rays
　　Regild yon ruined ha'.

Though fair be England's cultured plains,
    And green be Erin's Isle,
To me auld Scotia still retains
    The dear lo'ed mither smile.

Her trusty lads are leal and brave,
    Her lassies bricht and braw;
Their worthy sires are wise and brave,
    Their matrons kind to a'.

O Border Land! O Border Land!
    Ye'll aye be dear to me,
Frae distant isle, and foreign strand,
    My heart gaes back to thee.

HASTE THEE, O GENTLE SPRING.

A WEE bird sat on the topmost bough
    Of a tall and leafless tree;
Which the March winds swayed, while the sunbeams played
    O'er the birdie perched sae hie.

To gather the first of the fair spring flowers,
    I had knelt by the ivied wall,
When a melody sweet did my senses greet,
    'Twas the bird on the poplar tall.

And this was the song which the bonny bird sang,
  As he perched on that leafless tree,
Which the March winds swayed, while the sunbeams
    played .
  O'er the birdie sitting sae hie.

>
> Come, gladsome Spring,
> Thy sweet flowers bring,
> And scatter abroad with glee,
> Let thy light feet tread
> O'er the daisies' bed,
> From their deep sleep set them free.
> With the magic wand
> In thy fairy hand,
> O haste thee over the lea,
> And change the scene
> To the emerald green
> So pleasing and fair to see.
> On these boughs undrest
> Let thy life-touch rest,
> And the clustering leaves shall hide
> Their bare gaunt limbs
> From the axe that trims
> Their forms to the woodman's pride.
> At thy welcome call
> The song birds all
> Their sweetest lays shall sing;
> Their trysted mates
> For thy coming waits,
> Then haste thee, O gentle Spring.

The song was sung, and the wee bird flew
   Away o'er the flowerless lea,
But I sang again the sweet refrain,
   Which had found an echo in me.

For to some I love, this bright springtide
   Both flowers and nests will bring,
And their trysted mates now impatient waits
   Thy coming, O gentle Spring.

ETTRICK JEAN.

SWEET flowers bloom fair in Ettrick Vale,
   When simmer breezes roond them blaw,
There's roses red, and lilies pale,
   By shepherd's cot and lordly ha'.

But 'mang the flowers in Flora's train,
   There's ane I'd croon o' beauty queen,
A rose tae pu' I wad be fain,
   My peerless rose is Bonnie Jean.

Bricht lassies trip owre Ettrick meads,
   Amang the sweetly scented hay,
And mony a' swain at gloaming speeds,
   To serenade his rustic fay.

And when ahint the Weirdlaw hill,
   The gowden sun has sunk at e'en,
Then owre the muir, wi' heart and will,
   I'll hie to meet my bonnie Jean.

AUTUMN.

Dear Autumn's peaceful, pensive calm,
    O'er hill and vale is stealing,
Sweet evening sheds her dewy balm,
    Fair Nature's sorrow healing.
Yon silvery crescent, shrined in blue,
    A tender light is lending;
One golden star of palest hue,
    Night's royal maid attending.

Oh! would that I, sweet evening hour,
    Thy restful peace might borrow,
Oh! that thy gentle soothing power
    Could ease my heart's deep sorrow.
The careless world goes laughing by,
    With mirth and sounds of gladness,
Which I but echo with a sigh,
    A weary sigh of sadness.

My gentle mother laid to rest
    In yonder graveyard dreary,
Fain would I lay me on thy breast
    And stay my wanderings weary.
The light of home is glimmering low,
    There's nought but sounds of weeping,
And every heart is filled with woe,
    For thee, so calmly sleeping.

No more thy loving voice we'll hear,
   In vain our tears and sorrow;
But thou art safe from pain and fear,
   In Heaven's endless morrow:
Dear Autumn, peaceful, pensive, calm,
   O'er hill and woodland stealing,
On weary hearts distil thy balm,
   Till time completes their healing.

SEASONABLE WISHES.

To M. L.

Beautiful spring, with its gentle showers,
Its budding trees, and opening flowers,
Hope's sweet foretaste of joys to be,
E'en so be the days of youth to thee.

Beautiful summer, with roses crowned,
Scattering blessings on all around,
Gladsome and long, joyous and free,
Thus may thy life like summer be.

May spring and summer in thee combine,
And flowery wreaths of joy entwine,
Ever fresh and fair like the cheering spring,
May life to thee sweet pleasures bring.

ADRIFT.

I MOORED my bark in a sunlit bay,
My hopes were high and my heart was gay;
With a silken chain, and a silver key,
Love bound my boat to a stately tree.
But a storm arose, and the foaming waves
Engulfed my hopes in their watery graves;
My trust was firm in my stately oak,
But it swayed, and bent, and at last it broke.
Adrift, adrift on life's wide sea!
Adrift, adrift, ah! woe is me!

The night was dark, and the waves were high,
Not a star appeared in the murky sky,
As over the deep my bark was tossed,
And I cared not to live, now love was lost.
The morning broke o'er the inky deep,
And the sea-birds woke from their wave-rock'd sleep;
But every trace of the land was gone,
And I on the wild dark sea—alone.
Adrift, adrift on life's wide sea!
Adrift, adrift, ah! woe is me!

Darkest the hour ere the dawn of day,
And fiercest the fight which endeth the fray;
The wildest storm finds a peaceful calm,
And for wounded hearts time hath soothing balm.
A proud, strong will, in its maddening woe,
Defied the fate that had laid it low;

Rebelled, and strove, and tried to free
Its fluttering wings from its Lord's decree.
Adrift, adrift on life's wide sea!
Adrift, adrift, ah! woe is me!

But the tempest ceased, and the waves were stilled,
And I saw it was good what the Father willed.
Then a peaceful joy o'er my spirit crept,
And the angels watched while I calmly slept.
They moored my bark in a sunlit bay—
My angel guides o'er the sea's highway—
And I woke with my heart once more at rest,
For I knew that the Father's will was best.
No more adrift on life's wide sea,
But anchored safe, dear heaven, in thee.

GARNERED SUNBEAMS.

DREAMING o'er those secret treasures
    In my scented writing-case—
Withered flowers and old love-letters,
    With souvenirs from many a place.
Useless rubbish!—yet for me
    Priceless relics—which I keep
For the memories which they waken,
    Though those memories make me weep.
Not in sorrow—for the pain
    Of the partings long ago,

Which I felt so bitter then,
   Give not now one pang of woe.
But the happy days of youth,
   Which have flown so swiftly by,
Leaving but these dead mementoes
   Of the past, till I, too, die.
Seem again to flit before me,
   Bright with sunshine gay with flowers,
Gilding with their sunny radiance
   Many dark and lonely hours.

BONNIE NELL.

THERE dwells a maid by Ettrick side,
   The bonniest lass I e'er hae seen;
The forest flooers in a' their pride
   Could ne'er surpass this rosy queen;
The modest violet breathing sweet,
   The rosebud, and the heather bell,
Before their rival fair retreat,
   And yield their charms to bonnie Nell.

When simmer wore her mantle green,
   And flooers shed perfume on the air,
Amang yon bosky wuds at e'en,
   I met young Nell, my winsome fair.
That faultless form and modest look
   Enthralled me with love's mystic spell;
Her beauty first my fancy took,
   But virtues bound my heart to Nell.

The snaw lies white on Weirdlaw Hill,
    The wind blaws cauld oot owre the knowe,
It whistles eerie round the mill,
    And drifts deep wreaths to ilka howe :
But what care I for driftin' snaw ;
    For let the blast be e'er sae snell,
I'll tak my plaid and haste awa'
    Across the muir to see my Nell.

SCOTIA.

    SCOTIA ! my native land,
    Girt by thy mountains grand,
Home of thy son's hearts, where'er they be ;
    Matchless in summer time,
    Rich in thy mellow prime,
Snow-capped and winter-wrapped—bride of the sea.

    Clasped in that ocean arm,
    Scotia fears no alarm ;
Enthroned at Dunedin, majestic sits she.
    Rightful her royalty,
    Yet leal in her loyalty,
Scotland, unconquered, maintains her degree.

    Land of our buried sires.
    Land of our fond desires
Home of thy son's hearts, where'er they be ;
    Still shall thy poets sing
    Till all the echoes ring,
Scotland the beautiful ; Scotland the free !

EDINBURGH.—Acrostic.

EDINA, home of Scottish hearts,
Dear to thy sons where'er they be,
Invincible to warlike arts,
No envious foe shall conquer thee.
Behind yon sheltering castle walls
Our kilted lads their vigils keep,
Unwearied they when duty calls,
Ready aye, while others sleep.
Grand Dunedin, Scotland's pride,
Heaven's blessing with thee bide.

MUSIC AND POETRY.

ENNOBLING music, highest art;
   Dear poesy—sweet sisters twain—
Without thy charms the human heart
   An earth-bound groveller might remain.
O remnant of fair Eden's bliss,
   Devotion's offering, meet for Heaven,
Thou sweet'ner of life's bitterness,
   Thou priceless gift to man, God-given.
Orient light that radiates
   Coruscant beams through heart and mind—
Hail love divine, that delegates
   Exultant music to mankind.

THE DAYS O' YORE.

My dear auld hame, my dear auld hame,
    'Mang Ettrick hills sae green,
To see thee now, or hear thy name,
    Brings saut tears to my een.
Far, far frae thee, sweet Ettrick Vale,
    My weary feet hae strayed,
Yet dear to me thy flowery vale,
    Where I in childhood played.

Thy moorland knowes and mossy nooks,
    Thy woodlands wild and weird,
Thy foaming falls and flowing brooks,
    By memories sweet endeared.
But the auld hoose, the theekit hoose,
    That stood on yonder brae,
Is noo a braw new dwelling douce;
    The change aye maks me wae.

The smiddy stands where then it stood,
    The burnie wimples by,
The bairnies yet in merry mood
    Sport 'neath the cloudless sky;
But a stranger strikes the anvil noo,
    And strangers' bairnies play
Beside the burn, that ripples blue
    On this fair summer's day.

For soondly noo the auld folks sleep,
    Frae a' life's sorrows free ;
Nae mair they work, nae mair they weep,
    And hushed their halesome glee.
The auld folk, the dear auld folk,
    Weel lo'ed in days o' yore ;
Now unkent faces, smiling, mock
    My spierin's at their door.

The Ettrick winds adown the vale,
    The breezes softly blaw,
Wild flowers still deck the bonny dale,
    But the charm has left them a'.
The auld kirkyaird, the auld kirkyaird,
    It's mair than hame to me,
Since they for whom I fondly cared
    Sleep 'neath the auld yew-tree.

LADY MAY.

OH, Allan, spare my breaking heart,
This night for ever we must part ;
Within my breast the poisoned dart
Of anguish pierces deeply, O.

Allan—Why should such grief thy bosom pain,
    Why should my love be all in vain ?
    If I thy prizéd heart retain,
    Why wilt thou then forsake me, O ?

Lady M.—My father's pride of high degree
    Forbids this dream of bliss to me;
    Forbids me e'en to think of thee,
    As if I could forget thee, O.

Allan—Alas, my lowly birth ye scorn;
    To share my humble cot ye mourn;
    A mask of love thy pride hath worn,
    The stranger's heart to conquer, O.

Lady M.—Fain would I share thine humble lot,
    Contented in yon lowly cot;
    To me 'twould be a charmed spot
    Where'er my Allan lingered, O.

Allan—Then I must bid thee sad farewell,
    To all my hopes the burial knell;
    Yet once again, my darling, tell
    Thou wilt not soon forget me, O.

Lady M.—No fleeting, fancied love is mine,
    My changeless heart shall e'er be thine,
    Until my darkened life decline,
    And daisies bloom above me, O.

Allan—Sweet Lady May, thy tears restrain,
    Thy lover is no shepherd swain,
    But Lord of yonder proud domain
    Is he who kneels before thee, O.
    Consent, thy noble parents yield
    That I their fairest flower may shield
    With fondest love, in yonder bield,
    The Castle of Balmearie, O.

THERE CAM AN AULD MAN.

THERE cam an auld man awooin' to me,
A leal auld man, and a laird was he,
He thocht that a dainty wee wife I'd be,
Sae he made up his mind to marry, O.

He bade me come yont and see his big hoose,
Where a' thing was braw and cosily douce,
And the laird at the fireside sittin' sae croose,
Was sure that na langer I'd tarry, O.

But little forsooth did the auld man ken,
That my heart was far in yon highland glen,
That I'd raither hae love, in a but and a ben,
Wi' Ronald Macdonald, at Cruachan, O.

Sae the laird he may wait, or wed as he wills,
For cauld is the wooin' awantin' love-thrills;
In yon ivy-wreathed cot, amang the green hills,
I lo'e, and be lo'ed by my laochan,* O.

THE BRIDGE.

ON the moss-grown wall of the bridge I sit,
    And list to the murmuring stream;
Through the shimmering leaves, the sunbeams flit,
    Like the bright thoughts in my dream.
But my heart is heavy and sad to-day,
    And my spirit would fain be free,
From the fettering bonds of its curbing clay;
    And the wearifu' dool I dree.

* Gaelic, meaning hero.

Yet here as I sit on the moss-grown wall,
    And list to the murmuring stream,
Through the shimmering leaves the sunbeams fall,
    Like the bright thoughts in my dream.

As I think of one in the far away,
    'Mong the lowland valleys so green,
Where the merlin cheers with his sweet-voiced lay,
    One heart 'mid the rural scene ;

And that heart I know has a thought for me,
    As it lists to the merlin's song,
'Tis a heart that is noble, and warm, and free,
    A heart that will love me long.

And here as I sit on the moss-grown wall,
    To muse by the murmuring stream,
Through the shimmering leaves the sunbeams fall,
    Like this bright thought in my dream.

GRIEF.

How can I laugh when my heart is sad?
    How can I sing when the tears will flow?
Smiles are for those whose hearts are glad,
    Songs are for those who feel no woe.

But 'tis hard to part with ones we love,
    To bid them a long or last farewell ;
To meet no more till we meet above,
    Than vainly I strive my grief to quell.

To feel that the love which cheered my life,
    Is lost and can never be found again ;
To struggle alone 'mid the toil and strife,
    And no one to care for my sorrow or pain.

Then ask me not to join in your mirth,
    But leave me alone with my grief awhile ;
'Twill wane with the love which gave it birth,
    And then, as of old, I may sing and smile.

JEANIE.

Jeanie come list, as a song I twine,
Around thy name, dear cousin of mine,
Now in the prime of life's summer day,
Evergreen joys at thy feet I'd lay.
Scented flowers from the groves of mirth,
Where perfumed springs from the soil hath birth,
Opening buds of the pink-hued rose,
Rich as the cheek where the bride blush glows,
Dear emblem of love, 'mid life's thorny cares,
Maidenly garland modesty wears ;
Gather them soon, ere they withering fall—
A life without love, is no life at all ;
Link then in the wreath, with a golden ring,
Another name, and again I'll sing.

A SILVER WEDDING.

BRING a silver crown for the matron bride,
As she stands once again by her husband's side,
She is wed anew with the silver ring,
And her children the bridal offerings bring.

There are silver threads 'mongst her raven hair,
And the rose hath paled on her cheek so fair,
Her form hath tint its once willowy grace,
But contentment beams in her smiling face.

On her husband's brow is the touch of time,
He hath changed, since beneath the flowering lime,
They plighted their troth in the long ago,
To tread life's path amid weal and woe.

But unchanged their love since the days gone bye,
When they pledged their faith 'neath that summer sky;
What though wintry storms have around them blown,
Affection's bonds have but stronger grown.

May calm browed peace now their steps attend,
May health, and wealth, to their comfort lend,
Long life, and joy, to them both be given,
And a welcome home, at the gates of heaven.

CRADLE SONG.

Hush thee, my darling,
   Hush thee asleep,
Bright angels around thee
   Sweet vigils shall keep.

Pure is my flower bud,
   Unsullied by guile,
Like the glance of a sunbeam
   So joyous her smile.

Fair as May morning
   Beam her blue eyes,
Reflecting the shade
   Of yon azury skies.

Sleeping my loved one
   Peaceful and still ;
Angels watch o'er her,
   Guard her from ill.

BESSIE.

Only a baby fair, calmly asleep,
Safe in our Father's care—Why do ye weep?
Only a budding flower folded at night,
Closing at evening hour, to ope with the light ;
Only an angel guest, with thee awhile,
Back now to heaven's rest, untainted by guile.

Waiting at heaven's gate for thee to come,
Only a while to wait, then all at home.
Home in the better land, troubles all o'er,
There an unbroken band, partings no more.

TO MAJORIE.

To thee, my dear one, on thy natal day,
    What shall I wish?
If all that I could wish to thee were given,
With countless blessings I would strew thy way,
    And make thy life a glad foretaste of Heaven.

But earth is not our home, and pilgrims here,
    We journey on
Unto that better land of endless bliss.
Beyond this vale of tears, of sin, and fear,
    Where glorious reigns the King of Righteousness.

Then may each day, and all thy passing years,
    But bring thee nearer
To celestial bliss, and peaceful rest above;
No suffering there, no grief-impelling tears,
    The fullness there of joy, and perfect love.

Yet, on thine earthly path may joys abound,
    And sweet content abide,
May every good upon thy steps attend,
Like fragrant flowers, may blessings spring around,
    And cheering love with constant friendship blend.

CLADICH BURN.

(Tune.—"Kelvin Grove.")

Come wi' me to Cladich Burn,
  Bonnie Mary, O!
When the simmer days return,
  Bonnie Mary, O!
When the woods and braes are green,
When the wild rose decks the scene,
Come wi' me at dewy een,
  Bonnie Mary, O!

Where the falls are foaming free,
  Bonnie Mary, O!
With a blithsome laughing glee,
  Bonnie Mary, O!
Where the joyous din to hear,
Sounds like music to the ear;
Where the amber pools are clear,
  Bonnie Mary, O!

The flowery banks are fair,
  Bonnie Mary, O!
And the fern is growing there,
  Bonnie Mary, O!
The bower-enshadowed stream,
Where the sunbeams glint and gleam,
Looks a lovely fairy dream,
  Bonnie Mary, O!

We will visit lone Kilchurn,
  Bonnie Mary, O!

Then gae doon to Cladich Burn,
    Bonnie Mary, O !
The Isles of blue Lochawe,
Are the fairest e'er ye saw—
Ye will see them ane and a'.
    Bonnie Mary, O !

LOVE LONG AGO.

SOFTLY the moonbeams are falling around me,
    Revealing dew diamonds in hedgerow and tree,
Gently the breezes through leafy shades sighing,
    Awaken dear memories, my first love, of thee.

Hast thou quite forgotten, or dost thou remember,
    Bright evenings like this, in the long long ago,
When fondly we strayed 'mongst the dew-laden roses,
    When love vows were plighted in whisperings low ?

Ah me, for the future we painted so gaily !
    Ah faithless, and foolish, so soon to mistrust ;
When jealousy gained us to list to her treason,
    Love soon lay a-bleeding full low in the dust.

Not a farin the past, may be it was better,
    Those dreams were dispelled, now forgotten by thee,
Yet to-night I am dreaming again the delusion
    Of first love's sweet summer to thee and to me.

EXPERIENCE.

The longer we live the more we learn,
  And fools, by experience, wise men grow,
Not in vain are mistakes, if more clear we discern
  The light from the shade, which their dark shadows throw.

With sunshine around us, and friends by our side,
  Who smilingly flatter, and fondly caress—
How little reck we that such angels oft hide
  Only butterfly wings 'neath their hypocrite dress.

Their disguise, like their friendship, may last for a season,
  Should the sun o'er our fortunes continue to shine;
But the clouds of adversity mirrors their treason,
  And teaches us lessons we fain would decline.

Here, then, lies the shadow, but yonder 'tis brighter,
  For when false friends forsake us, we discover the true,
And who has not felt, how the burden seems lighter
  When a friend in our need appears 'mong the few.

In life's sunny morning we think not of terrors,
  And fear not the pitfalls which lie in our way,
'Tis only when later, repenting our errors,
  We learn the mistakes which beclouded our day.

If age could renew its fair youth like the eagle,
  And start from sweet childhood to live life again,
Would not we shrink back, though our birthrights were regal,
  If our past life experience we might not retain.

Yet children we are, till the veil be uplifted
  Which conceals from our spirits the mysterious unknown,
When worlds, by their Maker, like wheat shall be sifted,
  Then wisdom eternal shall clearly be shown.

MY LITTLE ONE GONE.

Sleeping, my little one, sweetly asleep,
So peaceful thou seemest, thy slumbers how deep,
Awaken, my darling, to thy mother who weeps,
Her tears on thy bosom thy snowy shroud steeps.

Sleeping, my little one, oh, thou art fair,
Still life-like the smile, which thy ruby lips wear,
And snowy thy brow, as thy garments above,
Where thy spirit hath fled to a Saviour's love.

Sleeping, my little one, calmly at rest,
Thy tiny hands folded upon thy dear breast,
Oh, why do I grudge thee thine early found bliss,
Why should I thus weep as thy dead face I kiss?

But oh, thou wert mine, and I held thee so dear,
No love like a mother's no kinship so near;
I know thou art safe, and I know it is well;
Yet, knowing all this, my heart will rebel.

I strive to be calm, and I try to submit,
And I pray for the grace which in time I shall get;
But awhile I must weep for my little one gone,
To that new-made grave in the churchyard lone.

EVENING DREAMS.

I'M waiting by the gate, love,
    Whilst the dewy shadows fall,
My heart awaits thy coming love,
    In love's expectant thrall.

I listen for thy footfall, love,
    That step so firm and light
I wait to hear thee whisper low,
    A loving last good night.

I'm waiting by the gate, love,
    O'er which the roses climb,
The summer breeze the fragrance steals
    From yonder flowering lime

Night's golden crown is gleaming love,
    Earth's dewy gems are bright;
And the beating of my heart, love, 's
    The only sound to-night.

I'm waiting by the gate, love,
    Where oft we met of yore,
But ah, in vain I linger now;
    Thou comest nevermore.

Yet still I wait, and fondly dream,
    Enwrapped by memory's spell,
And list to hear thy well-known voice
    Low whispering love's farewell.

ISABEL'S LAMENT.

ALAS! that summer flowers should fade,
   Or sunny hours e'er leave us, O ;
The greenest leaves are all decayed,
   And norlan' blasts now grieve us, O.

Ah! woe is me, that summer's fled,
   My aching heart is weary, O,
For e'er the trees again are clad
   I'll lie fu' low, and eerie, O.

Sweet summer brought restoring health,
   But winter's cauld will blight me, O ;
No kindly arm, no love, nor wealth,
   Shall save, when death shall smite me, O.

I fear not death, nor yet the grave,
   Nor dread to look beyond them, O ;
Though at my feet their waters lave,
   I have not yet bemoaned them, O.

But love is sweet, and friends are dear,
   And earth is fair and pleasing, O ;
The parting thought impels a tear,
   My pent-up sobs relieving, O.

O foolish me, like this to weep,
   For earthly joys uncertain, O ;
O'er sunlit braes the shadows creep,
   So cloud-like cares dishearten, O ;

In every bitter there's a sweet,
   Some comfort in each sorrow, O ;
And this my hope, again we'll meet,
   To spend an endless morrow, O.

MY BONNIE MARY.

The boatie rocks down by the pier,
    Nae mair the breezes blaw contrairy;
The silvery mune is shining clear,
    Then come wi' me, my bonnie Mary.
I'll row ye roond by Cladich shore,
    And owre tae lone green Innishail;
Among yon ruins ivied o'er,
    We'll list the seabirds' eerie wail.

The evening star's reflected beam
    On fair Loch Awe is sweetly shining;
The murmured music o' the stream,
    Is wi' the woodland sighs combining.
The boatie rocks doon by the pier
    Nae mair the breezes blaw contrairy;
The silvery mune is shining clear,
    Then come wi' me, my bonnie Mary.

We'll big a bower on this dear Isle,
    'Mang rowan shades that fleg the fairy;*
And ye will cheer me wi' your smile,
    My ain, my artless, bonnie Mary.
The boatie rocks doon by the pier,
    Nae mair the breezes blaw contrairy;
The silvery mune is shining clear,
    Then come wi' me, my bonnie Mary.

---

* It is an old Highland superstition, that the fairies or witches will not approach a dwelling near which is growing a mountain ash.

THE STORM.

'Twas summer, and the scorching sun
Oft o'er the cloudless heavens his course had run ;
Beneath his fiery gaze the flowerets drooped,
And nature, faint and languid, stooped.

In yonder furrowed field, the sun-burnt swain,
Oft leaning on his hoe some rest to gain,
And with his checkered 'kerchief wipe the sweat
Wherewith his aching brow is wet.

Yon angler wearied with his ill-success
To tempt the scaly tribes from their recess,
Now hies him to the leafy glade
To rest beneath some cooling shade.

Where on a mossy couch outstretched he lies,
And sleeping, dreams he wins the finny prize ;
So dream we oft, of noble duties done,
But, heedless, let the precious moments run.

Soon, as in answer to a prophet's prayer,
A cloud appears, a tiny speck that bears,
Impregnant in its fleecy form,
The sleeping nursling of the storm.

Fed by an unseen hand the cloud increased,
Till from its darkening midst there sprang released,
The Storm Spirit, in a lightning flash—
Swift herald of the thunder crash.

Then as the darkness deepened round,
And Night her mantle's folds unwound,
The tempest forth in its fury burst,
And none to contend with its raging durst.

Like the glimmering light of the breaking morn,
The incessant gleam put the night to scorn,
As the meteor flash with its tinted ray
O'er the landscape shone like the light of day.

How feeble the boasted power of man,
Mark the ruddiest cheek, how it waxes wan ;
Now awe-struck and silent the bravest quakes,
When the voice of the Lord the mountain shakes.

'Tis a glad relief when the long night o'er,
The morning breaks on the day's bright shore,
When the dark clouds melt, 'neath the softening beams,
And wearied watchers have peaceful dreams.

A SEANCE.

ONE night on the borders of dreamland,
    As 'twixt sleeping and waking I lay ;
I heard thy dear voice softly calling,
    To the regions of fancy away.

As the lark from the dew-laden heather,
    Up-springs the fair morning to greet ;
So unfettered and free rose my spirit,
    To realms where kindred souls meet.

A Seance.

And there in sweet spirit communion,
    We wandered together a space,
In that land of celestial beauty,
    Which science and art cannot trace.

Was it fancied, or real, now I wonder,
    This waking impression of mine ;
Could it be that my thoughts of the moment,
    Were reflected and echoed in thine?

Untrammelled by earth and its sorrows,
    Can we rise to the purer sphere ;
Not Heaven, not earth, yet between them,
    Where spirits inspired may appear.

Where genuis alone is triumphant,
    Where truth in her temple sits crowned ;
Where poesy weaveth her garlands,
    Where earth-fettered souls are unbound.

To some such emotions seem folly,
    To us they are holy and real ;
When weary with life's sin and sorrow,
    How soothing this blissful ideal.

Afloat in the ether of fancy,
    Looking down on life's care-troubled scene ;
We discern that the dark clouds are fleeting,
    And the bright sun still shining serene.

AN OLD MAID'S SOLILOQUY.

HEIGH, but its lone, sirs,
    To be an old maid ;
Now I'm fifty, ochone, sirs,
    There's no hope, I'm afraid,

That I'll ever be married,
    By youthful or old,
Too long I have tarried
    For acres and gold,

Which never were proffered,
    Though I've waited so long,
I refused what was offered,
    So am left to my song.

Och ! I'm weary of sitting
    Where so often I've sat,
All alone with my knitting
    And tortoise-shell cat.

I'm really so lonely,
    That to whisper the truth,
I wish that I only
    Had wed in my youth.

Then of lovers I'd many,
    Now, alas, I have none,
Here unthought of by any,
    I'm sitting alone.

My hair once so brown
   Is now scanty and grey,
And the roses have flown
   From my cheeks quite away.

Now wrinkles appear
   Where dimples once smiled,
And lone I sit here
   Without husband or child,

To whom might be dearer
   Those silvern threads,
Who would clasp them yet nearer
   Than golden-hued heads.

Heigh! but its lone, sirs,
   To be an old maid,
Now I'm fifty, ochone, sirs,
   There's no hope, I'm afraid.

FRIENDSHIP'S FAREWELL.

Ere to Edina's busy haunts ye bid farewell,
   Accept I pray, affection's tribute from my pen,
Amid the scenes ye seek, where loved ones dwell,
   Wilt thou forget? or wilt thou now and then,
By memory's magic lamp, retrace again
   Some pleasant moments in Edina spent

With friends, who will with fondest love retain
    Remembrance of the joy thy presence lent?
That word adieu breathes sadness in its tone,
    And often leaves a void which nought can fill
In weary, loving hearts left all alone,
    Whose troubled depths no balm can ever still.
To every scene of life congenial friendship adds a charm,
    Enhancing all the joys that on our steps attend,
Soothing our sorrows with affections warm;
    Spirits akin that with each other blend,
Devoid of flattery's gilded poisoning sweets,
    Yet rendering all their earned meed of praise,
With mild reproof affectionately entreats
    Pursuance of the bright reward in wisdom's ways.
Such only is a friendship worth the name:
    Firm as a rock, it stands the test of time—
In sunshine, shade, or gloom, 'tis aye the same,
    Unchanged by distance, sphere, or clime.
Let such a friendship, then, be ours to keep
    Untarnished by the flight of time or change:
Let pleasant memories wake and sad ones sleep,
    No slanders ever let our love estrange.
May all life's purest joys be thine,
    Success upon thy footsteps follow fast;
And ever shall this prayer for thee be mine—
    In heaven's better land a home at last.

A HIGHLAND LASSIE.

I met her in the glen yestreen,
The fairest lass that I hae seen ;
Love aimed a dart frae her black een,
Which wounded me fu' sairly, O.

As lithe and gracefu' as the deer
That drinks at yonder stream sae clear,
Wi' shy light footsteps drawing near,
When morning dews lie pearly, O.

Sae coyly came this artless maid,
When gowden eve began to fade,
When twilight crept adoon the glade,
And daisies e'en were closing, O.

Her cheek the rose's tint had stown,
The sun had kissed her dusky brown,
Her raven locks waved rippling down,
A swan-like neck disclosing, O.

A gaily checkered tartan plaid
The maiden's dainty shoulders clad,
Love-token frae some Highland lad,
Acceptance, hope begetting, O.

Sweet lassie met in yonder glen,
Whose name and hame I ne'er may ken,
Adorning now some but-and-ben,
Thou'dst grace a gowden setting, O.

LATRELLE.

LATRELLE sits lone i' the old grey tower,
  With a way-worn look on his face,
A grief-cloud rests on his high white brow,
  The wherefore, I would I might trace.

To lay my love at my hero's feet,
  I fain in my heart would go,
To share in his sorrows I then might hope,
  But maidens must never do so.

O why, O why are we fettered like this?
  Can the rules of cold etiquette bind
The love which wells from the deep heart-springs,
  And flows through the maiden's mind.

Bright laverock lend me your wings awhile,
  That I from the cloudless blue
May trill some lay, that will cheer and bless
  That dear heart, kind and true.

O sweet rosebud on the dewy spray,
  Had I but the grace of thee,
I'd breathe my wish to the western wind
  Which stealeth thy sweets with glee:

Then I'd bid the breeze on its errand fly
  To yon tower so old and grey,
To whisper a tale in somebody's ear,
  That would drive all his cares away.

THE PLEASURES OF FANCY.

Worn with sickness, care, and sorrow,
  Nought to comfort, none to cheer ;
Longing for some glad to-morrow,
  When dark doubts shall disappear.

All around me, dark and dreary,
  Low'ring clouds their shadows cast,
While my spirit, sad and weary,
  Ponders ever o'er the past—

Not upon my childhood's pleasures,
  Sweet although those memories be ;
But the days of youth hath treasures
  Dearer far than these to me.

Ah, these days of sunny gladness,
  Gilded with Hope's radiant gleam,
When no shades of care nor sadness
  Clouded young love's happy dream.

Ere the morning freshness vanished
  From the dewy wreaths of day,
Ere the noontide's sun had banished
  Glistening gems from hawthorn spray.

Whilst the perfumed breezes, stealing
  Fragrance from the dewy flowers,
Bore the song-bird's notes, revealing
  Nests half hid 'mongst leafy bowers.

Those the days in memory cherished,
  Summer's glow e'er winter's gloom,
And although the flowers have perished,
  Yet withering, shed they sweet perfume.

And oft, upborne on fancy's pinions,
  Visit I those scenes again ;
Forgetting in her bright dominions,
  All my sorrows, griefs, and pain.

IVY.

OVER yon ruin so gaunt and grim,
  The evergreen Ivy creeps :
Its deep-hued leaves, so glossy and green,
  Through the shattered wall daintily peeps.

Concealing the scars which storms have left,
  Filling the voids produced by time ;
Every crevice and crumbling cleft
  Restoring to beauty, and youth-like prime.

E'en so to the choice of her constant heart,
  The affection of woman will cling ;
And nought to its object will ever impart,
  The joys which that fond love can bring.

WEALTH *Versus* POVERTY.

They tell me that riches bring troubles and care,
    That few are both wealthy and good,
They tell me 'tis better to dine on poor fare,
    And dwell in a cottage though rude.

Yet somehow or other I can't quite agree
    With what those advisers protest ;
Their words may be true, but it still seems to me
    That wealth, though with troubles, is best.

'Tis all very well from a distance to scan
    The picturesque homes of the poor,
To romance o'er the life of some nobled-souled man,
    Or the grinning content of a boor.

But dwell for awhile in that ivy-clad cot,
    And share all the comforts therein,
Sympathise with the sorrows that fall to the lot
    Of its members, through sickness or sin.

When that dearly loved one pined slowly away
    For lack of support, and good skill ;
'Mid their anguish and tears, on her funeral day,
    Go mark their sad fears for the bill ?

To labour is good when our hearts are made glad,
    With the blessings of hope and sound health,
But how often when sick, or heavy and sad,
    We long for the comforts of wealth.

To work when the pulses are throbbing with pain,
    And sorrows nigh breaking the heart ;
With cares and misfortunes oppressing the brain
    And no hope which might solace impart.

Then tell me not of the trouble wealth brings,
    Since the antidote comes with it too,
Whilst the hearts that grim poverty cruelly wrings,
    Are helpless their bonds to undo.

LURLINE.

I LOVE to watch the willows
    As they bend across the stream,
As they kiss the tiny billows
    In the sunlight's silver gleam.

I sit and watch the willows,
    And I listen to the stream ;
But a deeper feeling mellows
    My pleasant waking dream.

A face of sunny brightness,
    'Neath a cloud of golden hair,
A step of fairy lightness,
    Seems to haunt me everywhere.

Lurline.

Oh ! gentle footsteps stealing
    Into this heart of mine,
Its deepest founts unsealing
    With those ruby lips of thine.

Say, canst thou ever bind again
    The love thou hast set free :
Shall all my pleading be in vain
    When love is all my plea ?

No, no, I cannot think that one
    So gentle and so fair
Could e'er possess a heart like stone,
    Or doom me to despair.

Oh ! could I hear that sweetest voice
    Low whispering "I am thine";
Oh then, my own, my only choice,
    What raptures should be mine.

I sit and watch the willows,
    And I listen to the stream,
But this deeper feeling mellows
    My pleasant waking dream.

NIGHT.

Alone at midnight's silent hour,
   A dreamy vigil here I keep;
Blest balmy slumber sits in power
   E'en night-wrapped nature seems asleep.

No sound the soothing silence breaks,
   Far distant seems the shaded hill;
My restless spirit only wakes,
   It's day-born thoughts pursuing still.

This peaceful hour's enduring calm,
   Unbroken by life's toiling din,
Distils a sweet and soothing balm,
   That lulls to rest the strife within.

Yon radiant gems that gleam afar
   From darkest depths of midnight sky,
With magnet power each golden star
   Updraws the thoughts to God on high.

With soul entranced, my raptured gaze
   Deep fixed upon the sea of night,
Discerns beyond the filmy haze
   Eternal beams of heavenly light.

Down through the dark, unfathomed space,
   Those glorious rays are streaming bright
A light from Zion's holy place,
   To guide the angel's earthward flight.

Unnumbered hosts descending, speed
    On wings of love to Adam's race,
Through 'wildering paths our steps to lead,
    And guide us to our Father's face.

They bring the weary wanderer back,
    They mould the wayward will ;
And, pointing to their homeward track,
    They whisper—" Peace be still ".

KATIE'S SECRET.

FARE ye weel, Donald Gary, ye've ta'en my heart wi' ye ;
    Noo dowie and downcast I'm sitting alane ;
O, could I but ken in return that ye lo'e me,
    The pairting wad tint the sair half o' its pain.

Were yon glances, sae tender, bestowed on me only,
    Or are the same tae ilk lassie ye see?
I wonder if now ye are feeling how lonely
    Without ae dear lo'ed ane the world can be.

Why did ye no tell me afore that we pairted,
    That true to your trysting ye'd hae me remain?
Sae leal tae ye, laddie, I'd be waiting true hairted,
    But noo I maun marry the laird o' Kilgrain.

Alas! for puir lassies their love maun lie hidden,
    And locked in their hearts till the day that they dee,
Unless that the lo'ed ane comes boldly unbidden,
    And opens the door wi' love's patented key.

ASLEEP.

Night's soft shadows fall around me ;
　　Evening dews begin to weep ;
Long the day has been in waning,
　　Now I'm weary—let me sleep.

I have watched the grey dawn breaking,
　　O'er the mountain's rocky steep ;
Watched the noontide's lagging moments,
　　Till I'm weary—let me sleep.

In the summer sunset gleaming,
　　Bright appeared yon ancient keep ;
Now the darkness veils its beauties,
　　And I'm weary—let me sleep.

But, mother, why those looks of sorrow ?
　　Brothers, sisters, how you weep !
Am I dying ? tell me truly ;
　　I'm but weary—let me sleep.

Sleeping, sleeping, sweetly fair ;
　　Wrapped in slumbers ; ah ! so deep,
She will wake ; no, never more,
　　From that long and dreamless sleep.

THE BORDER LADS.*

On the far-famed slopes o' the Eildon hills,
'Mang the gowden knowes, and the rippling rills,
Frae their ringing hammers, and the din o' their mills,
    Were gathered the lads o' the Border.

Here the gallant sons o' the souters brave
Let the flag o' Flodden aboon them wave,
They'll haud their ain, wi' the Border lave,
    The stately flowers o' the forest.

Then hurrah, hurrah, for our Border lads,
Wi' their braid Scotch bannets, and their black cockades,
The kilted clans wi' their tartan plaids,
    May meet their match on the Borders.

There's leal loyal hearts frae Teviot side,
Of their worthy sires the hope and pride,
Auld Scotland's foes they ne'er could bide,
    But ready, aye to defend her.

And braw, braw lads frae Gala banks,
Sae fu' o' fun, and wildish pranks,
But they'll win the day, and their country's thanks,
    When Britain needs her warriors.

Then hurrah, hurrah, for our Border lads
Wi' their braid Scotch bannets, and their black cockades,
The kilted clans wi' their tartan plaids
    May meet their match on the Borders.

* Written when the Border Volunteers were encamped at Melrose.

MOONLIGHT MEMORIES.

When Luna's soft and silvery light
    O'er nature casts a mystic spell;
When brightly gleam the gems of night,
    And whispering breezes secrets tell.

'Tis in this still and peaceful hour
    Our thoughts on fancy's pinions soar;
And memory wakes with magic power
    Recalling scenes in nights of yore.

The bye-gone years in misty haze
    Fleet cloud-like past before the mind,
Revealing to our wistful gaze
    The joys of youth left far behind.

And through these years the golden chain
    Of love and friendship glitters bright:
Each shining link portrays again
    A face once gazed on with delight.

In fancied forms they seem so near,
    We, half-forgetting, think to clasp
In fond embrace those held so dear
    Or meet their hands in fervent grasp.

Delusive dream, for nevermore
    Shall some, once dear to us, return:
Their feet now tread the golden shore
    Where ever lasts the nightless morn.

A few in distant climes now roam,
    And years have fled since last we met ;
With strangers some have found a home,
    And in new loves, our love forget.

But yet on moonlight nights like this
    'Tis pleasant to retrace anew
Our paths through life, and warmly bless
    Those constant ones who still are true.

COME TO THE WOODLANDS.

COME to the woodlands with me,
    Leave for awhile all thy cares,
Pleasures I'll lavish on thee,
    Joys which no sadness impairs.
Beautiful summer to greet,
    Loyally bow at her shrine ;
Violets bloom 'neath her feet,
    Her breath sheds a fragrance divine.

Dame nature thee calleth away,
    In the greenwood her revel she keeps ;
Then haste thee her mandate obey,
    E'er age o'er thy youthfulness creeps,
Then away to the woodlands, away ;
    Let mirth through the forest resound,
Away on this bright summer's day
    Where health and delight may be found.

ON THE RIVER.

Floating down life's troubled stream,
    Hand clasped in hand,
Wrapped in love's ecstatic dream,
Gilded by hope's golden gleam,
    Girt with faith's strong band.

Onwards down the rapid river,
    Heart answering heart,
Vowing love, and truth for ever,
None our wedded lives to sever,
    Nought but death us part.

Many a bark is on the river,
    Floating with the tide,
Far away they glance and quiver,
Disappearing soon for ever,
    Where the mists abide.

Youth and pleasure lightly sailing,
    O'er the placid deep;
Men, misfortunes sad bewailing;
Age, with boats all leaking, failing,
    Careless souls asleep.

I and thou, so close together,
    Wrapped in love's sweet dream,
On through fair and stormy weather,
Caring little, where or whither,
    Ends life's pleasant dream.

From love's spell, shall we awaken?
    Waken filled with pain,
Wake to find ourselves mistaken,
Wake to find our deep love shaken,
    Ne'er to rest again.

Or shall we our faith still keeping,
    All the years,
From our joys and sorrows reaping
Love's reward, till both are sleeping
    Free from fears.

Safe beyond the troubled river;
    On whose breast
Sin and sorrow surge for ever,
Where the faltering voices quiver
    Prayers for rest.

ISABELLE.

O the lady I love is bright and fair,
With a tinge of gold on her wavy hair;
I met my fay in yon birken wood,
With the violets twined in her silken snood.
My lady has eyes of the softest brown,
My peerless queen, with the violet crown,
Like a graceful fawn, or a wild gazelle,
Is my own, my beautiful Isabelle.

O, the lady I love is fair and bright,
And her fragile form is lithe and light ;
To the dingle dell, with a gentle speed,
Trips her dainty feet o'er the daisied mead.
As the nectar drop which the wild bee sips,
Was the dewy sweets of my lady's lips,
When beneath the stars, in the flowery dell,
I won the heart of my Isabelle.

ROSES.

The scent of the roses steals sweetly to me,
And breathes in their fragrance remembrance of thee,
Remembrance of thee, love, sweet memories of thee,
The scent of the roses is bringing to me.

Again 'mong the flowerets we wander at e'en,
Ere night's dewy curtain is drawn o'er the scene ;
Once more in the moonlight we lingering stray,
Again o'er the heather we roam far away.

With the scent of the roses there steals back again
Sweet memories of pleasure, sad memories of pain ;
But the dearest of all recollections to me
Is remembrance of thee, love, remembrance of thee.

Do I ever forget thee ? no darling, no, no,
When winter lies dreary, or June roses blow,
There blooms in my bosom, a floweret true blue,
"Forget me not," dear one, it blooms but for you.

SUNLESS DAYS.

THERE are sunless days, when the soul is sad,
When all the joys, and the good we had,
    Seem lost to us evermore,
When friends prove false, or when foes prevail,
And we stifle the sound of the anguished wail,
    As our grief-wave breaks on the shore.

When the aching head, and the weary heart,
Feel sadly unable to bear their part
    In the work of the dreary day;
When we fain would rest from the thankless toil,
From the mocking pride and the wearing moil,
    Imposed by our kindred clay.

O sensitive heart, 'mid the searing strife,
Which blights the bloom of thine inner life,
    Faint not, nor fail, be strong
In faith and love to the loving Christ,
Who but seemeth awhile to delay His tryst,
    He will come for his own, ere long.

Then thy morn shall break, and the shadows flee,
And the sad dark past thou shalt clearly see
    In the noon-day light of His love;
And thy grateful heart shall His goodness praise,
For His guiding grace, 'mong the thorny ways,
    Which led to the home above.

ELWAND'S FAIRY DEAN.

The wintry winds hae ceased to blaw,
    The ice-bound rills are free,
And rosy simmer wreathed wi' flo'ers
    Trips owre the daised lea;
Fu' green are Gala's woody heights,
    Her flowery vales are fair,
But Elwand's sweet sequestered shades
    Are dear beyond compare.

Then tryste wi' me, my bonnie lass,
    My ain, my artless Jean,
And meet me, love, ere fa's the nicht,
    In Elwand's fairy dean.

Adoon the sheltering leafy glade
    The rippling burnie sings,
And wi' the warbling wild bird's note
    The echoing woodland rings.
But when the westlin' sun gaes doon,
    And evening shadows fa',
The soothing charm of gloamin' brings
    A peacefu' hush owre a'.

Then tryste wi' me, my bonnie lass,
    My ain, my artless Jean,
And meet me, love, ere fa's the nicht,
    In Elwand's fairy dean.

BIRTHDAY WISHES.

To B. M., *Wardie*.

THE autumn leaves are falling fast,
    And sunny summer's almost past,
The shades of eve close early in,
    Soon will the winter storms begin.

But yet with thee, it is the spring,
    The spring of life, when all is glad,
New joys to thee each day doth bring,
    No griefs hath made thy spirit sad.

And now on this thy natal day
    Accept the best wishes of my heart,
May heavenly light illume thy way,
    And sorrow's clouds from thee depart.

May health, and wealth, and peace be thine
    May many happy years to thee be given,
And may each birthday, stand, in time,
    A milestone on the road to Heaven.

ALWAYS.

CANST thou always love me truly?
    Wilt thou not forget that vow?
When the wooing days are over,
    Wilt thou love me then, as now?

Wilt thou not regret that ever
    We as more than friends had met?
After years of life together,
    Wilt thou not thy love forget?

Loving once, I love for ever,
    But unloved, 'twere death to live;
Filled with fancies, wilful, wayward,
    Couldst thou all those faults forgive?

Hast thou seen the ivy twining
    O'er yon stately forest tree?
In its weakness fondly clinging,
    Wouldst thou, thus, enshelter me?

Think amongst the friends thou lovest,
    If none dearer, yet, ye know,
Love, only love, my heart shall win,
    Canst thou then this love bestow?

DUNEDIN'S WELCOME.

WELCOME, Duchess of Edina,
    Welcome, lady, to the home
Of our noble Prince, who brought thee
    Far across the ocean's foam.

Heart-felt was the people's welcome
    To the sailor's lovely bride ;
Happy be the sacred union,
    Ever may true love abide.

But a Scottish welcome, lady,
    Yet awaits thee on our shores,
Where our ancient Holyrood,
    Opes for thee her royal doors,

Where Edina, queen of cities,
    Watches for thee, o'er the Forth,
There a loyal welcome waits thee,
    Lovely Lily of the North.

THE WINTER OF THE HEART.

DECEMBER'S snow lies drear without,
    The wind sighs sadly o'er the lea,
And in my heart broods care and doubt,
    The drearest winter that may be.

Poor gentle heart, your store of love
    Ye hoarded long with miser care,
Contented with your hopes above,
    Your hopes of Heaven, so bright and fair.

Ah, would that yet ye knew no more,
    Than heaven's love would have ye know,
No wreckèd peace would strew the shore,
    Where whelming tides of anguish flow.

Poor simple heart, ye gave your all,
    All that a heart like thee can give,
At love's behest, at duty's call,
    Ye gave your life, that love might live:

Your life, aye heart, ye gave it free,
    That better life ye should have kept
For heaven alone, who gave it thee,
    But love was king, and conscience slept.

The Winter of the Heart.

To one amongst the sons of dust,
   Ye gave a deep and trustful love,
Poor wounded heart, thy loving trust
   Returns like Noah's wearied dove;

Returns to God from whence it fled,
   Returns to rest in Christ again,
To Christ, whose heart with sorrow bled
   For thee, poor heart, so crushed with pain.

An earthly idol here ye sought,
   Ye sought, and found, and worshipped too,
An idol shrined in every thought,
   As something noble, good, and true.

Before that idol's shrine ye bent,
   Affection twined her choicest flowers,
Your hoarded love ye freely spent,
   Poetic wreaths adorned its bowers.

Mistaken heart, ye found at last
   Your trusting truth was all in vain;
Your wreaths of love aside were cast,
   Ye reaped the thorny crown of pain.

Sweet summer reigns in flowery pride,
   The fragrant breeze sighs o'er the lea;
And in my heart no doubts abide,
   The balm of heaven hath soothèd me.

A LEGEND.

A MAIDEN lingered i' the wood,
When twilight shades began to brood
   O'er mountain, stream, and vale ;
The maiden's step was free and light,
The maiden's eyne were blue and bright,
A maiden graced to cheer the sight
   Of dwellers in the dale.

But why when silent stands the mill,
When rural life is hushed and still,
   At twilight's pensive hour ;
When evening stars begin to peep,
When bees and birds have gone to sleep,
Why should this maid lone vigils keep
   'Neath yon May-perfumed bower?

'Tis but a legend old I tell,
A heart enthralled by love's sweet spell
   The maiden's bosom shrines ;
And yonder, o'er the shadowy lea,
A comely youth I dimly see,
Now hastening to the trysting tree,
   As light of day declines.

A peaceful hour, a flowery shade,
An honest youth, a guileless maid,
   Two mutual hearts aglow
With young love's roseate flame ;
An earnest vow, a murmured name,
A maiden's yes, as answer came,
   In accents soft and low.

Life is not spent 'neath Maywhite bowers,
And few find paths bestrewn with flowers,
    And true love intertwined :
Yet life is not alone for toil,
The care and wear, and slavish moil,
Do soon the soul's white plumage soil,
    And numbs the heart and mind.

But earth hath pleasures, pure and gay,
And sweet is love beneath the May
    At twilight's peaceful hour ;
Then sit ye not in cheerless mood,
Nor on your cares and burdens brood,
For every ill there's equal good
    Within our will and power.

IN MEMORIAM.

" Blessed are the pure in heart."

A sleep in Jesus, peaceful rest,
N o rude awakings shall molest,
N o troubled dreams shall scare ;
E ternal rest, eternal gain.

L ife free from sorrow, sin, and pain,
O ! bliss beyond compare,
W hy should we weep for those asleep?
E manuel's blessed care.

Died 27th May, 1881.

A FLORAL OFFERING.

To Mrs. Mary Mackellar.

Fair poetess, I fain would twine
   A flowery wreath for thee ;
Although no flower, nor wreath of mine
   Fit for thy brow may be.

The queenly rose, I first would bring,
   As emblem meet of thee ;
Entwined with snowdrops of the spring,
   White flowers of purity.

The pensive lily, let me wreath
   With fragrant eglantine ;
And from thy native hills, the heath,
   With bluebells let me twine.

An amaranth, unfading love,
   Do thou accept from me ;
And hearts-ease, sprinkled from above
   With dews of peace for thee.

Unchanging friendship, ivy leaves,
   With these sweet flowers I'd twine
Poetic offering, fancy weaves,
   To lay at Mary's shrine.

MOTHER.

ACROSTIC.

M y rhyming wreath, let me entwine
O 'er thy name, sweet mother mine,
T hou to me art dearest still,
H aving thee, I fear no ill,
E ver warm, thy constant love
R eflects affection's source above.

A HAPPY NEW YEAR.

WHEN nature dons her wintry garb,
   And decks with icy gems her form,
The change but adds a varied grace—
   Majestic, now she rules the storm.

Though loth to part with sunny hours,
   Yet winter brings glad Christmas cheer;
And genial friendship ever warms
   To wish again a good New Year.

May the New Year now at our doors,
   Have many joys in store for thee,
And through its changing seasons bloom
   The flowers of truth and constancy.

May friends increase, and foes be few,
   May many happy years to thee be given;
And o'er thine earthly pathway beam
   The guiding light that shines from heaven.

YE MINSTREL'S TRYST.

TEN minstrels met i' ye greenwoode shade,
    Quhan ye foreste was fayre to see,
Ande ilke was clad i' ye tartane plaide,
    Ye garbe ofe his owne countrie.

And ten goode harps, on ye gowanie swarde,
    Were laide downe carefulie,
Ilke harp was a gifte to ye worthie barde,
    Frome ye goddess ofe poesie.

Some ofe ye minstrels were grey ande olde,
    Ande some ofe them fayre and younge,
But ye heart ofe a minstrele ne'er grows colde,
    While ye harp owre his breast is slung.

Ande quhan at ye e'enin' ye sun sank lowe,
    Ande ye veteran minstrele sang,
His words were tinged wi' ye roseate glowe,
    Whilk ye westlin' sunbeams flang,

Not onlie a minstrele true, was he,
    But a statelie warriour bolde,
A patriot, proude ofe his own countrie,
    As ye chivalrious knights ofe olde.

Then a dark-browed barde 'mid ye minstrele thronge
    Swept ye chords ofe his deep-toned lyre,
And sang ye power ofe enobling songe,
    'Till he wakened a kindrede fire.

In ye list'ning hearts ofe his compeers nine,
    As they sate 'neath ye greenwoode tree;
More power hath songe, than ye rosiest wine,
    To make minstrel's blude dance free.

Ande ye gentle maiden frome Peebles sang
    Ofe her sailor lad on ye sea,
Till ye echoing depths of ye foreste rang
    Withe ye sweet-toned melodie.

Uprose then a tall ande a grey-haired sage,
    Ye laureate barde was he;
Withe skill, ande ye rights ofe experienced age,
    He counselled them earnestlie;

To shun ye snares ofe ye tempting cup,
    Withe its deadlie alluring smile,
Seeking ever to win ye fallen, up
    Frome ye tyrannous tempter's wile.

A dark-eyed barde ofe a dreamie looke,
    Sang a simple ande touching laye,
Ye noble poore, as a theme he tooke,
    Withe their victories daye by daye.

A gifted youthe from ye Teviot's side,
    Sang ye joys ofe ye rural scene,
Whilk all shoulde seek in ye summer tide,
    'Mang ye glens ande ye mountains grene.

A worthie son, ofe ye minstrel's sire,
    Struck ye notes ofe a stirring strain,
'Till ye music wilde ofe his magic lyre,
    Made ye woodlands echo again.

And one sang well on that sacred theme,
  When a sorrowful Saviour wept,
'Mid ye garden's gloom, by ye Kedron's stream,
  While His sorrowful followers slept.

Then ye maid ofe Ettrick softlie sang
  Ofe friendshipe warme ande free,
Till ye creeping shadows ye gloamin' flang
  Owre bourtree bush, and lea.

For ye sun had sunk, ande ye e'enin' stars
  Beamed brighte in ye blue serene;
Ande ye minstrels thought ofe their homes afar,
  'Mang ye hills and ye valleys grene.

But they made them ye tryste, to meete again,
  By ye ruins of ye olde Abbie,
To sing ye songs, ofe ye joy ande pain,
  Attuned by their minstrelsie.

THE FLOWER OF GLENSHEIRA.

BRICHT rose the mune owre the brow o' Benvorich,
  Green 'mang the waters, lay lone Innishail;
Dark were the shades on the druid's fair island,
  Where Colin was wandering, dejected and pale.
And aye as the saft breeze sighed sad 'mang the oak trees,
  It bore owre the waters this mournfu' refrain,
Since faithless is Flora, the flower of Glensheira,
  The sun on young Colin shall ne'er rise again.

The Flower of Glensheira.

Sweet Flora was fair, as a rosebud in summer,
    Young Colin the pick and the wale amang men,
In childhood, they'd played 'mang the blue bells thegither,
    In youth, they had plighted their troth i' the glen.
But now as the saft breeze sighed sad 'mang the oak trees,
    It bore owre the water this mournfu' refrain
Since faithless is Flora, the flower of Glensheira,
    The sun on young Colin shall ne'er rise again.

To the Highlands came Randolph, the heir o' Braidmeadows,
    Frae the south o' the lowlands, to Glensheira came he,
And there he met Flora, the fairest of maidens,
    And she has consented his ain bride to be.
And sae as the saft breeze sighs sad 'mang the oak trees,
    It bears owre the water this mournfu' refrain,
Since faithless is Flora, the flower of Glensheira,
    The sun on young Colin shall ne'er rise again.

But down by Bouvouie, came Flora at midnight,
    Escaped from the bonds which her parents compelled,
There, borne by the saft wind, came Colin's sad ditty,
    And soon to his bosom the maiden was held :—
Sae now as the saft breeze sighs sad 'mang the oak trees,
    It bears owre the water this gladsome refrain,
Since faithful is Flora, the flower of Glensheira,
    Our bridal shall be ere the mune rise again.

MY RING.

PEARLS and rubies, pearls and rubies,
    In your delicate gold-work enshrined ;
Pearls and rubies, pearls and rubies,
    With the love of two hearts interwined.

Pearls and rubies, pearls and rubies,
    Round is the circlet ye wreathe,
Pearls and rubies, pearls and rubies,
    No ending hath true love but death.

Pearls and rubies, pearls and rubies,
    Binding together we twain,
Pearls and rubies, pearls and rubies,
    Ne'er to be sundered again.

UNCERTAINTY.

LONELY I sit by the sea-shore, waiting,
    Watching the waves as they ebb and flow,
As they gently swell from their watery dell,
    To kiss the beach with their lips of snow.

Watching the strangers who heedlessly pass ;
    Waiting for one that never may be,
Beneath the blue wave may-hap is his grave,
    Or cold as those strangers his heart to me.

O for true tidings of sorrow or joy,
    To tell me, my lost one, of thee :
To watch thus and wait, not knowing thy fate,
    Is wringing the heart-life from me.

MY HEART CLINGS TO THEE.

WEIRDLY the winter winds sigh round my dwelling,
    And eerie the sough that comes up from the sea,
Alone, and so weary, with sad bosom swelling,
    I feel, love, how fondly my heart clings to thee.

'Mid gay scenes of pleasure, I've mingled, all smiling,
    And fair to the flatterers who gathered round me,
With mirth, and with music my sorrow beguiling,
    But ah, love, beneath it, my heart clung to thee.

O why should I love thee so, blindly forgetting
    That man is inconstant, and likes to be free
To sport with the syrens his pathway besetting,
    It may be, yet fondly my heart clings to thee.

Cruel and cold were the words that were spoken
    By lips that should only breathe kindness to me,
In wrath, worse than folly, our deep vows were broken,
    Yet ever my own love, my heart clings to thee.

My heart clings to thee, my heart clings to thee,
    I try to forget thee, I strive to be free,
In vain is my struggle, wherever I be,
    In joy and in sorrow, my heart clings to thee.

MY AIN LAD.

O this is no my ain lad,
   Braw though the laddie be,
Na, this is no my ain lad,
   The lad that loes but me.

Though this braw chiel has gowden rings
   On his white fingers sma',
And though his coat be superfine,
   His sarks like driven snaw;
Yet brawer in my e'en, I trow,
   Is Donald's auld grey plaid,
And dearer far the hame-spun claith,
   On his young shoothers braid.

Na, this is no my ain lad,
   Weel cleedin though he be,
He'll ne'er be like my ain lad,
   The lad that's dear to me.

This toon-bred youth has gentle speech,
   And woos wi' langidge fine,
He tells me o' his hoose sae grand,
   And a' that would be mine,
Gin I'd consent to gae wi' him,
   And leave my hieland hame;
As well might he yon wild bird cage,
   And think to mak it tame.

Na, this is no my ain lad,
   Rich though the laddie be;
I wadna' leave my ain lad,
   For a' that wealth could gie.

Nor wad I leave my hieland hame
    For his toon-house sae braw,
I'd raither hae my Donald's love,
    Than servants at my ca'.
Sae gang your ways, my dainty chiel,
    Ye ne'er my lad can be,
I couldna' leave my native glen,
    Nor wad I gang wi' thee,

Nor wad I gie my ain lad
    For a' the lads I see,
Sae weel I loe my ain lad,
    And he loes nane but me.

FRIENDSHIP.

AROUND our thorn-entangled paths of earth,
    Blooms there some fragrant flowers, to cheer, and bless
The home-bound pilgrim, hungering 'mid the dearth
    Of joys enduring, until he gain the bliss of Paradise.

One beauteous flower, with leaves deep-green bedight,
    Sheds perfume sweet o'er those who finding, prize
And treasure it with care and wise delight :
    A healing plant, which blooms 'neath darkest skies.

Thus fair friendship roots, and flow'ring, ripens
    In the rich soil of human sympathies,
And noble loves : e'en when sorrows deepen,
    Distilled comfort, springs from pure heart-unities.

MY WEE WIFIE.

IN yon bonny glen, I hae biggit a hoose,
    A bonny wee hoose, wi' a lum i' the riggin ;
Wi' a spade i' my hand, I'm singin' fu croose,
    As the yairdie, wi' pleeshur, and tent, I am diggin'.

Last yule tae my hoosie I brocht a wee wifie,
    The bonniest wee flower that grew by the Yarrow,
Sae modest and coy, yet blithesome and lifie,
    She's my winsome bit lassie, my true-hearted marrow.

There's braw lads in Yarrow, and lassies fu' bonny,
    Though nane wi' my Jeanie could ever compare ;
And aye when I think, she preferred me tae ony,
    My heart gaes a stoun o' love, amaist sair.

My peerless wee jewel, the croon o' my life,
    Nae ither can e'er hae a nook i' my heart,
To love and to cherish my darlin' wee wife,
    Shall be my endeavour, till death us do part.

ALONE.

Alone, alone in life's wide wilderness,
    No hope, no joy, no gladness comes to me;
My verdant hopes and joys, chill grief hath seared,
    No genial spring revives the blighted tree.

Alone in spirit, evermore alone,
    No answering heart re-echoes to mine own;
In silence, hearing life's dim destiny,
    Waiting the hour when God's way will be shown.

Yet all is well, amid the darkness deep,
    Often I hear sweet angel voices nigh,
Softly whispering, " Courage, all is well,
    The Father knows ". Then my soul rejoices,

Rejoices then with joy ineffable,
    Surpassing all the joys that pleasure gives;
Alone, nay, not alone, for One is here,
    And ever with me, my Redeemer lives.

OUR OWN.

As o'er the world we wander wide,
   Or sail from shore to shore,
Joy thrills the heart, to clasp the hand,
   Of some dear friend of yore.
But, though mankind our brethren be,
   And kindness should be shown,
Our bosom's inmost core we keep,
   Aye sacred for our own.

The noblest hearts can love the most,
   Love holds o'er all its sway,
The holiest bond on earth is love,
   And love shall live for aye,
Yon infant, on its mother's knee,
   (Life's tiny bud unblown),
Is more than all the world to her
   Who calls it now her own.

The fertile Indies may be fair,
   Bright France may gaily smile,
But dearest to the British heart,
   Is England's sea-girt isle,
Then courteous be to all mankind,
   For kindliness be known,
But sacred still your bosom keep,
   For those ye call your own.

THE CAMERONIAN'S DREAM.

By Ettrick's gentle stream, a dwelling stands,
Embosomed 'mid dark pines, and silvery birch,
A pleasant picture ; and within there lived
An aged elder, of good Cameron's creed ;
An honour to that martyr's honoured name,
Nathaniel-like, there seemed in him no guile.

Now on his dying bed the elder lay ;
And while the western sun shed glowing light,
Before he passed to shut day's golden gates,
The old man slept in child-like restfulness,
But when the last ray kissed " dark Wardlaw's " brow,
And evening shadows crept slow up the vale,
The elder woke, and gazed with wondering look
Around, as if his spirit lingering still
'Mid visions fair and bright, had not yet filled
Its earthly home with soul intelligence :
Awhile his eyelids closed, and then he spoke,
In low and earnest tones, with hands enclasped :—
" Come, till I tell thee what I saw, and heard,
For though those weary eyes of mine shall close
In death's deep sleep, ere many suns shall set,
Yet, thou art young, and if thy days be long,
Thine eyes may see fulfilment of my dream.

" Upon a mountain side methought I stood,
Surrounded by unnumbered hosts of men,
From every clime they were, of every creed,
United in one name, ' the Sons of God,'

And in our midst, stood one of kingly mien,
Whom, by the nailprints in His hands, I knew;
O'er 'Shiloh's Prince' a snow-white banner waved,
Whereon, with blood inscribed, 'Redemption' gleamed,
No warlike weapons in our ranks were seen,
But open bibles in all hands were held,
No battle cry arose to stir the air,
But in a psalm, of God-won victory,
And heart-felt joyous praise, our voices joined
In one great burst of deep-toned melody.

"Whilst on the mountain side were gathered thus,
All who worshipped Christ, in heart sincere,
Upon the plains beneath great legions stood,
Our foes; of Antichrist, the followers,
Now, armed, they wait the expected conflict,
Anticipating conquest o'er Christ's Church,
Yet powerless to advance, till *He* should bid.

"But lo, when rose that psalm of victory,
Some strange commotion stirred the hosts beneath,
And wild confusion surged in war-trained ranks;
In vain, commanders shout, their voices add
But to the mingled discord and alarm:
Amongst themselves, their keen-edged swords they wield,
Brother 'gainst brother, friend 'gainst friend, they fought,
Till dead and dying strewed the reeking plain.
Then came the remnant, and at Jesu's feet
Laid down their armour, and besought His grace,
Nor did they seek in vain, for freely given
Was pard'ning mercy from the Prince of Peace.

"Thus was our victory won, by God alone,
Our God, in whose hand are the hearts of men;
And though to us be given the conqueror's bays,
Low at His feet, before the sapphire throne,
We'll cast our crowns, and worship evermore
In the glad presence of our mighty King."

But three more suns had set, and now again
The glowing west was radiantly bright,
Casting a golden glory o'er the vale;
Then came the angels for the good man's soul,
Guiding its upward flight to Paradise.

AWAKEN.

Awaken, O sleeper, the day is at hand,
    The morning of truth dawns on thee,
The light of the gospel is gilding the land,
    From the darkness of slumber be free.

Awaken, O sleeper, the noontide is past,
    How long wilt thou dreamily sleep?
Arise, lest with clouds the sun be o'ercast,
    Or night-shadows stealthily creep.

Awaken, O sleeper, the night cometh on,
    While yet there is mercy, awake,
Ere yet from God's justice thy sentence hath gone,
    Arise, and thy slumbers forsake.

Alas, foolish sleeper, thy sun is now set,
    And mercy hath shut to her door,
The dank dew of death on thy brow lieth wet,
    The morn breaks for thee nevermore.

MARY.

I HEARD the angels singing,
    Last night, when Mary died,
I caught a glimpse of glory,
    And my darling glorified.

As they bore my lov'd one upwards,
    Through the dark and silent night,
I traced the heav'nly strangers,
    To the golden gates of light.

Up through the shades of darkness,
    They sped in their noiseless flight,
Shrined in a cloud of glory,
    Robed in the spotless white.

More faintly fell the music,
    As they neared the distant goal,
Where countless hosts were waiting,
    To welcome the earth-freed soul.

A burst of light celestial
    Gleamed o'er the darkness wide,
When the door of Heaven opened,
    And the veil was drawn aside;

Drawn aside for a moment,
    When my darling's name was sealed,
But only angel lips might sing
    Of the glories then revealed.

The door was shut, and the night-cloud fell,
  As dark as it lay before,
And all of earth, I loved, was gone,
  And to me would return no more.

Yet I could not weep o'er the lifeless clay,
  So fair in its perfect mould,
I could only think of the spirit's home,
  Within those gates of gold.

She was all I had in the world to love,
  And it may be I loved too well,
My anguished grief, as I watched her fade,
  I strove, for her sake, to quell.

Now the bond is severed which held me here,
  And the world hath no charms for me,
I can only wait with expectant joy,
  The hour which shall set me free.

THE MOTHER AND HER BOY.

A DARK-EYED boy, by his mother's knee,
  Repeats a text from the Holy Book,
The mother's eyes in her darling's see
  A somewhat grave and troubled look.

"Mother, what means those words I learned,
  About being partakers of perfect rest?"
(The mother's heart o'er her lov'd one yearned,
  As close to her dying couch he pressed).

"You told me, mother, that Heaven above,
   Had gates of pearl, and streets of gold,
And that all who on earth our Jesus love,
   Shall dwell with Him in that beautiful fold.

"But, mother dear, if they rest all day,
   And the day so long, when there is no night,
I'd get wearied, mother, and want to play;
   Would the angels tell me it was not right?"

The mother smiled as she kissed her boy,
   And told him again of the beautiful land,
Where no pain, nor toil, shall our peace alloy,
   Where rest remaineth at God's right hand.

The child went out to his mirthful play,
   The mother lay still on her couch of pain,
But her spirit went forth on its heav'n-ward way,
   And the little one heard not her voice again.

  *   *   *   *   *   *   *   *   *

An aged man on his dying bed,
   In child-like slumbers lay,
Like a halo over his pillow shed,
   Gleamed his thin locks, silvery grey.

The soothing charm of a soft light fell
   O'er the sleeper's tranquil brow,
Where the furrowed lines, the record tell
   Of life on a brave ship's prow.

His children's children around him stand,
   With their parents now grown grey,
A little one touches the old man's hand,
   (His mother-named favourite, May).

The old man woke with a gentle smile,
   And said, as he kissed her brow,
" Good bye, sweet May, for a little while,
   My mother calls me now ".

Then weeping friends around him pressed,
   And he blessed them one by one,
"Weep not," he cried, " I long for rest,
   I have laboured from sun to sun ".

They laid him down 'neath the yewtree's shade,
   Near his mother's grave so green,
'Mid tears, and grateful honours paid
   By his country and his queen.

THE MASTER IS COMING.

The Master is coming, prepare for thy guest,
   Let thy household in readiness be,
Let the tables be spread with the finest thou hast,
   For to-night He shall sup here with thee.

The sanctum of conscience examine with care,
   That all there in order may be;
To the chamber of memory often repair,
   Of *that* door, thy Lord keepeth a key.

In the chambers of fancy, what pictures are seen?
   Are they fit for the Master to see?
All-searching His gaze, no curtains may screen
   These hidden thoughts, painted by thee.

In thy wonderful soul-house ascend to the dome,
   To the chambers of reason and mind,
Give diligent heed that their God-stamped home,
   Well furnished, and pure, He may find.

The Master is coming, prepare for thy guest,
   Let thy household in readiness be,
Let the tables be spread with the finest thou hast,
   For to-night He shall sup here with thee.

BY MOONLIGHT ALONE.

Beneath the fair moon's silvery light,
   I love to wander o'er the hill,
How sweet the peaceful calm of night,
   When all around is hush'd and still.

Where purpling heather decks the brae,
   And golden broom adorns the fell,
Amongst their wilds, I wend my way
   To yonder green and dewy dell.

Like moonlit diamond, gleams the spring,
   From whence this tiny brooklet flows,
Encircled with an emerald ring,
   The crystal fount its lustre throws.

The sparkling dewdrops gem the spray,
   And glitters 'mongst the sleeping flowers,
The brooklet murmurs on its way,
   Through mossy nooks, and leafy bowers.

A timid hare, upspringing, speeds
   With noiseless footsteps up the brae,
And startled fancy quickly breeds
   A hundred thoughts of elf and fay.

Beneath the fair moon's silvery light,
   When next I wander o'er the hill,
I prithee, puss, keep out of sight,
   Your presence nearly made me ill.

EPISTLE TO H.

My clever, warm-hearted brither,
I doot if nature had anither
    'Mang a' her stock,
To match the sample bard she sent us,
    Afore she broke.

Atweel I gat your rhyming letter,
And sure am I, that no a better
    Wi' a' his talent,
Could Burns hae penned, even though he'd been
    "A Hawick callant".

I'm glad to hear ye're a' fu' weel,
Lang may ye a' be spared tae speel
    The brae o' life;
And may your pathways a' be clear,
    O' cares and strife.

Dye think this winter ere will end,
Or langer last? kind Heaven forfend.
    Or sune, fair simmer
May try in vain wi' leaves to cleed
    The sapless timmer.

Fu' oft' this weary winter time,
I've wished that in a sunnier clime
    My lot were cast,
For sair I dreed the piercing cauld
    O' norlan blast.

But O, my heart tae Scotia warms,
I couldna leave her sheltering arms,
      Though cauld her breath ;
Sae I maun bide me where I am,
      Though't be my death.

Gae kindly greetin' tae the bards,
Tae ane and a' my kind regards,
      Though far awa' ;
My warmest feelin's aye are wi' ye,
      I loe ye a'.

On kindly words that we should speak,
I read a lay the ither week,
      I' the Hawick paper,
And weel I trow oor sister fair 's
      Nae twinkling taper.

But e'en a strang and steady licht,
Wha lang will cast a radiance bricht
      On a' aroond,
O' these first notes frae her sweet lyre,
      I like the soond.

Noo I maun curb my halting rhyme,
And patient wait, the pleasant time
      O' postie's ring,
Which frae yersel, I hope, ere lang
      A note will bring.

A note, na, na, that's merely cant,
I want a lang melodious chant,
      On ocht ye like,

'Twill music be, it maitters not
    What chord ye strike.

Till then, guid nicht, and joy be wi' ye,
And gin we're spared, I hope tae see ye,
    Upon that day,
Amang the bards at Thornwood Ha',
    When comes sweet May.

March, 1878.

THE PURSUIT OF LIGHT,

AND OTHER POEMS ON SACRED SUBJECTS.

THE PURSUIT OF LIGHT.

From the burning sands of the eastern plains,
From the flowery west, where the summer reigns,
From the sunless land of eternal snow,
From the darkest depths of human woe,
The soul of man, by the gospel light,
Shall rise again to its pristine height.

Confined in a cage of moulded clay,
Which time defaces with grim decay,
The restless spirit strives or pines,
For an upward flight to holier shrines :
Fettered and bound by its living chains,
Polluted and vile with sin's dark stains ;
Banished afar from the spirit-land,
By the just decree of a sovereign hand,
In rebellious hate, or in trustful love,
It awaits the great tribunal above.

Where superstition rears her head,
Besprinkled o'er with rootless green ;
Where ignorance, so dark and dread,
May still in fruitless height be seen,
Between those hills of darkening power,
A village lies, o'er which they lour,
With sun-obscuring deadly might,
For which 'tis named, the vale of night,

From distant lands a preacher came,
A man of God, unknown to fame,
With pitying look, upon the height
He stood, and viewed the vale of night:
And while he gazed, his bosom yearned,
And holy zeal within him burned,
Here, gospel radiance to impart,
To every weary, darkened heart:
"How long," he cried, "shall error reign?
How long shall sin its power retain?
When shall the knowledge of the Lord,
Be spread o'er all the earth abroad?"
Haste now thy coming, righteous King,
And nations to thy footstool bring,
Arise, effulgent source of light,
And scatter all those shades of night.

Strong in the faith, the preacher strove
The people's hardened hearts to move;
Sin's everlasting death he taught,
With saving grace he them besought:
Of Jesus's love with tears he told,
And, like the saintly Paul of old,
He suffered toils, and stripes, and death,
With pardon on his latest breath.
Yet not in vain the good man's toil,
Though fruitless seemed the parchéd soil,
The seeds were sown that yet would bear
The harvest of his faith and prayer;
And sure, if gems for souls be given,
A starry crown he wears in Heaven.

The Pursuit of Light.

A youth of thoughtful, modest mien,
Near to the preacher oft was seen,
Though, when the pastor sought to find,
Some evidence of Lucien's mind,
Proud diffidence his thoughts concealed,
No inward yearnings he revealed,
But fled into the wastes around,
To muse upon the truth profound.

Like seed revived by summer rain,
Like sunshine o'er the golden grain,
The martyr's blood bedewed the soil
Of Lucien's heart : Where faithful toil
Had sown the Gospel message free,
In trust the harvest yet should be.

To leave the vale of brooding night,
To choose the path that leads aright,
To reach perfection at a bound,
To tread o'er Heaven-enchanted ground,
In sinless peace of mind to bask,
Young Lucien deems an easy task.

Experience youthful dreams dispel,
And for the dreamer it is well
If, in his inmost heart of hearts,
He stores the lessons she imparts.

So Lucien learned that troubles lay
Unnumbered in the narrow way,
That he who seeks to enter there,
Must take the shielding staff of prayer.

But yet to reach the distant height.
From whence came streaming rays of light,
The traveller must his strength apply
To find perfection ere he die.
Once at the Source of yonder Light,
No longer faith, but present sight
Shall guide him on in sinless peace,
To where all toils and troubles cease.

But, when the mountain top he gained,
His courage fell, his heart was pained ;
For, lo ! a higher mountain still
Demands his energy and skill.
A little while he silent stood
In disappointed, doubting mood ;
Then looking backward o'er his course,
And looking forward to the source
Of perfect light and life, he cries,
" Yet onward, upward, for the prize ".

Not misspent strength, not wasted toil,
Though steep to climb, though hard the soil,
The hills of knowledge yield a store
Of priceless gems in ancient lore,
Of golden fruits and fadeless flowers,
Which bloomed at first in Eden's bowers,
While from the table-land the views
With clear ideas the mind indues.

So Lucien climbed the hills of light
To reach perfection's envied height ;

But higher yet, and higher still,
Peak rose o'er peak, and hill o'er hill,
Each one seemed clearer than the last,
No cloud o'er it a shadow cast ;
But, when 'twas reached, a brighter far,
As morning sun to evening star ;
So glorious gleamed the distant steep,
He needs must reach it, ere he sleep.

But, lo ! an angel, in the way,
Who smiles, and answers Lucien, Nay,
Thou well hast toiled, and meekly striven,
To find, what thou shalt gain, in Heaven ;
For only there perfection lies,
It is the saints' immortal prize.

To live a pure and holy life,
Amid earth's scenes of sin and strife,
Is better far, than depths profound
Which scientific searchers sound ;
But, nearest to the throne above,
Are those, whose hearts o'erflowed with love ;
Yet, even these, 'twas only grace
That made them meet to gain that place ;
And through that grace, at Heaven's gate,
Man shall regain his first estate.

THE TWILIGHT HOUR.

"AT EVENING-TIDE IT SHALL BE LIGHT."

When the summer sun is sinking,
   In the golden glowing west,
Come sweet memories, dream-like linking,
   Through the twilight hour of rest.

Happy evening hours that lie
   In the distant dreamy past;
Ah me! how swift those moments fly
   Which we wish so long to last!

Youth, ambitious, onward hies
   To the noontide heat of life,
Panting for some gilded prize
   'Mid the turmoil and the strife.

But when shadows gather round us
   And the night begins to fall,
Mercy breaks the chains which bound us
   To the world's enslaving thrall.

At the nether threshold waiting
   For the call that bids us come,
Failing powers all indicating
   Nearness to the darksome tomb.

Then across the turbid river
   Brightly beams a holy light,
From the sun which setteth never
   In that land where is no night;

And its beauty, all celestial,
   Weans our raptured souls away
From the love of things terrestial,
   To the joys of perfect day,

Where an endless rest remaineth
   For the saints at God's right hand ;
There the King of Salem reigneth
   In that fair and happy land.

LIVE LOOKING TO JESUS.

WHEN the shadows of night are fleeting away,
And the lark is uprising to carol her lay,
Greeting the dawn of the new-born day,
Let thy praises ascending be accents of love :
Live looking to Jesus for light from above.

When the moontide hath scattered all traces of night,
And yon sun, in the glory and strength of his might,
Is blessing our earth with warmth and light,
Stand fast in the faith, with thy banner unfurled :
Live looking to Jesus, the light of the world.

When evening o'er nature her mantle hath cast,
And the day with its joys and its sorrows hath passed,
Be ready in time, this may be thy last ;
Prepare for the night, the night of the tomb ;
Live looking to Jesus to lighten its gloom.

When weary and worn, let this be thy rest,
Live looking to Jesus, and lean on His breast;
He is waiting to hear and grant thy request;
Whate'er be thy burden, however oppressed,
Live looking to Jesus and thou shalt be blest.

MY REFUGE.

The night is dark, the way is drear,
    Be Thou my guide;
From every danger, grief, and fear,
    Do Thou me hide.

The gathering clouds are low'ring nigh,
    O shelter me;
Thine arrows gleam athwart the sky,
    I trust in Thee.

My heart is filled with secret grief,
    And anxious care;
From Thee alone I seek relief,
    O hear my prayer.

My inmost thoughts Thine eyes can see,
    Yet not contemn,
I fearlessly look up to Thee,
    Though man condemn:

If, Lord, those clouds Thou lettest break
    Above my head,
Leave not my heart in fear to quake,
    Life's storms amid:

But be Thou present, and in peace
 My soul shall rest;
All inward doubts and dreads shall cease
 At Thy behest.

Be Thou my refuge and my guide
 Till life be o'er;
In Thee I trust, in Thee I hide
 For ever more.

GO TELL THY GRIEFS TO JESUS.

Go tell thy griefs to Jesus,
 When sorrow clouds thy brow;
Whate'er thine heart oppresses,
 Go tell it to Him now.

Tell not the world thy sadness
 It cares not for thy woes;
Tell not thy sorest trials,
 No secret griefs disclose.

But tell them all to Jesus,
 For He will sympathise;
His love shall soothe and rest thee,
 In Him thy succour lies.

He knows it all beforehand,
 E'en more than thou canst tell;
Yet waits He for thy coming,
 Thy dark doubts to dispel.

IN THE VALLEY.

Sick and wounded, Lord, I kneel;
Great Physician, Thou canst heal;
Grant, I pray, Thy soothing balm,
And my troubled spirit calm.

Weak and weary, let me rest,
Gentle Saviour, on Thy breast.
Strength and courage, Lord, impart
To my faint and fearing heart.

Poor and friendless, Lord, to Thee,
Friend of friendless ones, I flee;
Nought I seek of worldly cheer,—
All I have, if Thou art near.

Lord, Thy call with joy I hail,
Lead me through the darksome vale;
Till I reach the golden strand,
Blessed Jesus, hold my hand.

RETROSPECT.

Now the shades of night close round me,
    And the light fades in the west,
Let me linger here, and ponder,
    'Ere I lay me down to rest.

Retrospect.

Backward, o'er the day departed,
   Let me turn a searching gaze,
From the closing shades of evening
   To the morning's dewy haze.

Have I, through this day, been faithful
   In my blessed Saviour's cause?
Have I served the Master fully,
   Loved and kept His holy laws?

Have I truly loved my brother?
   Have I sought my neighbour's good?
Did I seek to follow Jesus
   As a true disciple should?

Have I sought to save the erring
   From a life of endless woe—
Pointing to the great redemption,
   All my heart with love aglow?

Have I shown a good example
   In my words and actions all—
Seeking to upraise the fallen,
   Mindful I am apt to fall?

Alas, alas! my conscious guilt
   Constrains my lips to answer, No;
My noblest thoughts but feeble are
   From which my words and actions flow.

My God, with Thee I humbly plead,
   Thy pard'ning mercy now extend;
Impart Thy grace to keep me pure,
   And guide me till life's day shall end.

FAITH, HOPE, AND CHARITY.

WHEN Faith unfettered heavenward flies,
Intent on some high enterprise,
Love lingers near, and Hope's glad ray,
Like Orient dawn presages day,
Inspiring dreams of joy in store,
And blissful life-cups running o'er!
Munificent as Heaven above,
Dear Charity! thy name is Love.
Hope waxeth faint, e'en Faith may fail—
Eternal Love shall aye prevail!
Reflector of the Father's mind,
All perfectness in thee we find.
Let Faith lead on, let Hope still cheer,
Divine-voiced Love hath cast out fear!

IN MEMORY OF JANET,
AGED 23.

I KNOW thou art laid in the garden of death,
   And loved ones are strewing sweet flowers on thy
      breast;
Peacefully hushed is the fluttering breath—
   Thy labour is done, thou hast entered thy rest.

Yet I cannot think of thee gone for aye,
   Since nearer and dearer thou seemest now
Than when, on that wintry parting day,
   I kissed thy beautiful snowy brow.

In Memory of Janet.

Ah, little I dreamt when I left thee then,
   And as little thou thought'st of it either, I ween,
That never below would we meet again;
   That ere my return thy grave would be green.

Bitter the pang that entered my spirit,
   When they sent me the tidings of sorrow and gloom;
Sadly I wept for the beauty and merit
   So early consigned to the night of the tomb.

I pictured the grief of thy husband and mother,
   When they laid thee to rest in thy dark narrow bed;
I thought on the tears of thy sister and brother,
   As they looked on the face of the beautiful dead.

But hope is triumphant, and faithful is He
   Who has borne thee hence from sorrow and pain,
In the mansions above, from sin thou art free;
   Then why should we mourn as if grudging thy gain?

In the dewy eve, as I thoughtfully sit
   And wistfully dream of the better land,
I see thee oft, as thou seemest to flit
   In ethereal light 'mid the angel band.

With a golden crown on thy sunny hair,
   And thine harp attuned to the holy song;
In the spotless robe which the ransomed wear,
   I see thee *one* of the glorious throng,

Then I long for thee—*not* to bring thee back
   To this weary world of darksome night,
But I seek more closely to follow the track
   That leads to thy heavenly home of light.

I.H.S.

I LOVE the name of Jesus,
    His words to me are sweet;
Oh, that I aye may listen,
    Like Mary, at His feet.

I have not heard His blessed voice,
    I have not seen His face,
Though oft within mine inmost soul
    His lineaments I trace.

I know His form is glorious
    His face divinely fair;
I know His love is boundless,
    And I that love may share.

I know His blood is cleansing,
    I know His grace is free;
I know He gave His precious life
    For sinners such as me.

To all that come unto Him
    He will acceptance give;
And whosoever cometh,
    For evermore shall live.

Beyond this dreary desert,
    In Canaan's happy land,
Our eyes shall yet behold Him,
    Enthroned at God's right hand

And when, earth's veil uplifted,
   We see Him face to face,
In joyful strains for ever
   We'll praise redeeming grace.

YONDER.

Beyond Death's gloom-wreathed portals
   Above yon star-gemmed sky,
Awaiting way-worn mortals,
   The fair possessions lie.

A home of peace and beauty,
   Where all is pure and fair,
No longer stern-browed duty,
   But sweet Love ruleth there.

Where earthly bonds are not binding,
   Where the fettered heart is free,
Where the gladsome years, unwinding,
   Encircle Eternity.

'MID THE SHADOWS.

WANDERING 'mid the shadows here,
Filled with doubtings, grief, and fear,
Longing for some ray of light
To illume our darksome night;
Jesus, Saviour, be thou nigh,
Listen to Thy children's cry.

Drinking of life's bitter cup,
Lord, come in, and with us sup,
Bitter draughts shall taste more sweet,
If we sit at Thy dear feet,
Jesus, Saviour, bend thine ear,
And thy children's sighing hear.

From Thy shining throne above,
Send some token of Thy love,
Bid the white-winged angels bear
Balm, to soothe each cankering care,
Jesus, true and living vine,
Graft us in, and keep us Thine.

All is drear where Thou art not,
Thy presence cheers the darkest lot,
All gracious thou thy mercies sure,
Unfaithful we, our hearts impure;
Lord, our consolation be,
Fix our trust alone in Thee.

HE GIVETH HIS ANGELS CHARGE O'ER THEE.

CHILDREN of Zion, why look ye so sad?
    Now through the wilderness wending your way,
Ye, 'mid the throng, alone should be glad,
    As homeward ye hie to the realms of day.

Is it the dangers of earth ye dread,
    The numberless perils by land and sea?
Fear not, but trust Him, these dangers amid,
    Who giveth His angels charge o'er thee.

Do cares and sorrows around thee press?
    Dost sigh for thy low and obscure degree?
Repine not, God loveth thee none the less,
    But giveth His angels charge o'er thee.

Is it from trials of spirit ye shrink?
    Tell it to Him on thy bended knee,
Think not 'tis the cup of His wrath ye drink,
    For He giveth His angels charge o'er thee.

Children of Zion, rejoice in your King,
    Trust ye His wisdom in every decree,
Up through the wilderness joyfully sing—
    He giveth His angels charge o'er me.

HOLY JESUS, KEEP ME PURE.

When the world, with syren's wile,
Would my wavering heart beguile,—
When its gilded joys allure,
Holy Jesus, keep me pure!

When at times my restless will,
Unrestrained by fears of ill,
Wildly seeks some worldly cure,
Blessed Jesus, keep me pure!

When dark grief my spirit shrouds,
When sore pain my brow beclouds,
When despair my hopes immure,
Blessed Jesus, keep me pure!

When death's shadow o'er me falls,
When nature sounds her warning calls,
Let Thy mercies, Lord, be sure;
Jesus, dying, keep me pure!

MY REDEEMER LIVETH.

Jesus, thou art my life, my light,
    My strength, and hiding place;
My guide, to lead my steps aright,
    My God, to give me grace.

Beyond all names, Thy name to me
    Is fraught with fragrant love;
To Thee alone I bend the knee
    In prayer, Thou hear'st above.

Jesus, when false all others prove,
    I closer cling to Thee;
No slanderous foes can ere remove
    Thy precious love from me.

Thou knowest, Lord, each wayward thought,
    My every act lies clear,
Yet, Thou hast with Thy blood me bought,
    Thine heart hath held me dear.

Lord, with Thy strength my weakness shield,
    And with Thy love me guard,
To no temptation let me yield,
    Be Thou my great reward.

FAR AWAY.

Dear ones 'neath the greensward sleeping,
        Far away,
Eyes, that now know naught of weeping,
Hands, the golden harp-strings sweeping,
        Far away;
Nevermore, ye care shall borrow
From some dreaded coming morrow:
Perfect peace, in place of sorrow,
        Far away.

Where pale grief can enter never,
        Far away;
Where no severed heart-strings quiver,
Where pure love abideth ever,
        Far away;
Where the saints are lowly bending,
With their angel guides attending,
Round the throne their praises blending,
        Far away.

Dear ones in the brightness dwelling,
        Far away,
Know ye aught of sad hearts' swelling,
Know ye aught of will's rebelling,
        Far away.
From the jasper walls of Heaven,
Unto you is it still given,
Hope to bring to souls unshriven,
        Far away.

Far Away.

From your homes of peace and glory,
        Far away,
Come ye with love's old old story,
To the wanderer grim and hoary,
        Far away ;
To the careless, seeking pleasure ;
To the miser, o'er his treasure,
When the last hour fills life's measure,
        Far away.

Pass ye through the portals golden,
        Far away.
By your angel guides upholden,
In your snowy robes enfolden,
        Far away ;
From your blissful homes descending,
And on earth-freed souls attending,
In their flight to Heaven ascending,
        Far away.

At the shining gates of Heaven,
        Far away ;
Unto you is it but given,
There to wait the tempest-driven,
        Far away ;
There to watch for tiny strangers,
Brought from mansions, and from mangers,
Brought away from earthly dangers,
        Far away.

Dear ones in the glory dwelling,
    Far away,
In your hearts pure joys are welling,
Joy, all thoughts of grief expelling,
    Far away.
Blessèd dead, in Jesus sleeping ;
Blessèd eyes, that know no weeping,
Blessèd hands, the harp-strings sweeping,
    Far away.

THE BIBLE.

God in His love this book hath given,
To guide us on our way to heaven ;
By faith we trust its truths divine,
Inspired by love, like gems they shine.

Whilst o'er earth's dreary desert way,
We journey on through life's long day,
God's word, like Israel's cloud, shall guide
Our weary feet till eventide.

And when night's darkening shadows close,
Death and the tomb, our dreaded foes,
Shall by this fiery pillar's light
Prove golden gates to glory bright.

HOME OF MY HEART.

Home of my heart in the far away,
Land of light in the realms of day,
O, when shall we see thee, dear country above,
O, when shall we drink at thy founts of love :
Hail blissful land, where no sin shall be,
Hail peaceful land, from temptation free,
No heart-sorrows lurk in thy fragrant bowers,
No thorns of care mid thy fadeless flowers.

Our earth is fair, but its beauties bloom
But to wither and droop to an early tomb ;
Our homes are blessed with affection's ties,
But death is here, and our loved one dies ;
Then we sadly sigh, or we wildly weep,
O'er the icy clay in its dreamless sleep,
And we linger long by the new-made grave,
While our hearts are far o'er the Jordan wave.

We watch by the gates of the closing day,
When the glory-gleams o'er the cloudlets stray,
And we watch by the shores of receding night,
To catch a glimpse of our home in light.
Let us wait and watch, let us watch and wait,
Till the angels pass through the pearly gate,
At the break of morn, or at setting sun,
They will guide us home, when our work is done.

CHARITY.

"Inasmuch as ye did it not unto them, ye did it not unto me."

Wearied and old,
   Hungry and cold,
      Out on the wold
         He wanders alone.

Night coming on,
   Far from his home,
      'Mong strangers to roam
         Friendless and poor.

None for him caring,
   Sorrows past bearing,
      Almost despairing
         Prays he for aid.

Then through the dark night,
   Beams there a bright light,
      Cheering his dim sight
         With prospects of rest.

Now onward he hies,
   Fresh hope in his eyes,
      Till comes he where lies
         A village of note.

At the door of the inn,
   'Mid the bustle and din,
      Without money or kin,
         Humbly he knocks.

Denied all admittance,
    He craves but a pittance,
        To secure him acquittance
            From hunger and cold.

No answer returned,
    Contemptuously spurned,
        With a coldness that burned
            His feelings with shame.

Onward again,
    Through the wintry rain,
        Seeking in vain
            For victuals and rest.

Pleading for food,
    Starving he stood,
        Yet none there that would
            But grant him a crust.

Fainting and ill,
    He sinks on the hill,
        Then all is still,
            Perished of want.

O England, if this
    Be the signs of thy bliss,
        There's something amiss
            With thy people and laws.

Thy Children need more,
    Than learning and lore,
        To reach yon bright shore
            Of glory and love.

Not learning, nor gold,
  Not treasures untold,
    Not a liturgy cold,
      Will aid, or suffice.

Upon that great day
  Of judgment array,
    If Jesus will say
      Depart ye from hence;

Unanswered before,
  I knocked at your door,
    But despising the poor,
      Ye lived at your ease.

Now depart to your doom,
  More dark than the tomb,
    For you there's not room
      In the mansions above.

AT THE GATES.

METHOUGHT I had reached the gates of heaven,
Upborne on the wings of prayer,
  And I heard the song of the angel-band,
  Of the blood-washed throng
  In the spirit land,
As I knelt enraptured there.

At the Gates.

And familiar tones I heard again,
Of loved ones gone before,
    As in joyful strains
    The hymn they sung,
    Of the Lamb who reigns
    The redeemed among,
Whom they worship evermore.

But I knew not their holy song,
For to me it was not yet given
    To enter the gates
    Of that city fair,
    (Where a welcome waits
    The ransomed heir,
To his glorious home in heaven.)

For my robes were defiled with sin,
And I dwelt in a house of clay,
    Though my prisoned soul
    In its wingless flight
    Had reached the goal
    Beyond death's night,
In the regions of endless day.

'Twas but a glimpse of the great unseen,
A sweet fortaste of His love,
    Who hath left us awhile
    Our place to prepare
    Where entereth nought vile
    Through the portals fair,
To the numberless mansions above.

O beautiful land, how I long for thee,
With thy holy beams of effulgent light;
    When this life is o'er,
    And the world hath passed
    On thy peaceful shore,
    We shall see at last
The morning break from the tomb's dark night.

REST.

Mid every scene of our changeful lives
    We seek for rest;
But we seek in vain, and each vainly strives
To reach the goal of his dreams of bliss;
Ah! fruitless hope, in a world like this
    By rest unblest.

On yonder shore of radiant light,
    Of joy and peace,
Where no sinking sun presages night;
No borrowed beams are needed there,
For the Lamb is the light of that city fair
    Where troubles cease.

O blissful rest, O perfect love,
    At Jesu's feet;
On wings of faith let us soar above
This weary earth defiled by sin,
From its pains and strife, from its restless din,
    To that rest so sweet.

FAREWELL.

There is a word we often hear,
   Which makes fond hearts with sorrow swell,
A note of discord to the ear
   Sounds in that parting word, farewell.

Everything of earth must perish,
   Nothing here can last for aye;
E'en the hopes we fondly cherish,
   Like misty shadows fleet away.

But the Christian's joy is lasting,
   For, though in the silent tomb
Loved ones may be calmly resting,
   Soon they shall in beauty bloom.

In that land where is no sighing,
   Where is heard no sad farewell,
Glad reunions and undying,
   Where the saints in glory dwell.

Thus, though for a time we sever,
   Though on earth we meet no more,
May we meet in heaven for ever,
   And the God of Love adore.

MISERERE.

Hail source of light, to Thee I cry,
From darkest depths, where low I lie,
Weak human reason flickering throws
But shadows grim of dreaded foes,
From which I shrink in wild affright,
Unknowing what is wrong, what right,
Yet wrestling ever with my doubts,
This one, then that, the other routs,
Till wearied with the constant strife
I'd gladly yield my burdened life.
With Thee I plead, let now be given
The sunless light that is of heaven,
Those holy beams which dazzle not,
Though no obscuring vapours float
Betwixt our gaze, and Zion's light,
Enthroned in Glory's highest height.
In Thee no darkness is, in us
Dark doubts arise, which we bemoan
As evils sent by Thee. Weak man,
To mete God's love by his brief span,
Man's love, a feeble flickering light :
God's love, the sun in noontide height ;
Man's life, one short illusive day,
God was, and is, and is for aye.

A BROKEN FLOWER.

Safe in her Saviour's keeping,
   Sheltered within the fold,
At rest in the grave is sleeping
   That form of beauteous mould.

But the spirit hath burst its prison,
   And escaped from its cage of clay,
And on joyful wings hath risen
   To realms of endless day.

No cankering grief is there,
   To blight the flower of her youth,
In that city so bright and fair,
   Abideth pure love and truth.

Safe from the tempter's wile,
   No more from her Father's home
Shall the flatterer, base and vile,
   Win her again to roam.

Safe from the taunting sneers,
   At rest from her toil, and grief,
From all her shame and fears,
   In death she hath found relief.

THE MEDIATOR.

We have an advocate with the Father.

Lord, when before Thy throne at last
  All nations shall appear,
When every thought and action past,
  Shall rise unveiled and clear ;
O, full of guilt, where shall we hide
  Our trembling selves from Thee ;
How shall we, Lord, Thy wrath abide,
  If once Thou angry be?
High and holy, true and just,
  Almighty God, and God alone,
We, the offspring of the dust,
  Gathered round Thy judgment throne ;
Moulded in Thine image good
  By the working of Thy hand,
Fair and sinless once we stood,
  In a fair and sinless land :
Disobedient to Thy laws
  Fell we from our first estate,
Who, in heaven shall plead our cause,
  While in silent guilt we wait ?
Who is this ? The Son of Mary,
  Hear those Jewish elders say ;
Who is this ? Opinions vary,
  Some have knelt to Him to pray,
Save us, save us, Lord, they cry,
  Son of David, wilt Thou hear?

Jesus, Son of God, most high,
    Save us from the doom we fear.
All too late their earnest pleading,
    Mercy's door is closed and fast,
Long for sinners interceding,
    Christ hath come as judge, at last.
Come, as judge, with condemnation
    To an unrepentant race,
Come with love and mediation,
    To all those who sought His grace,
See His flock around Him gather,
    Hear their Shepherd's gentle voice—
Come ye blessed of my Father,
    In His presence now rejoice.

THE GOOD SHEPHERD.

It is not the sheep, on the barren wold,
That seeks the Shepherd, or finds the fold,
But 'tis the Shepherd, who seeks his sheep,
And brings it back, in his fold to keep.

Wandering afar o'er the mountains wild,
A Father sought for his erring child,
And he found him at last in sorrow and pain,
Then he brought him back to his home again.

Out in the world to the wastes of sin
The Saviour comes, with His love to win
His wayward sheep to the peaceful fold
In the heavenly land, with its bliss untold.

Over the hills of our pride and hate,
The Father hastes, ere it be too late,
And finding us humble, and willing at last,
He takes us back, and forgives the past.

WEARIED.

I'M weary of the world's wild battle,
    Its surging waves of care and strife,
I'm longing for that peaceful haven
    The shadow of the tree of life.

I'm weary of the ceaseless toiling,
    Of bitter words, and searing jest,
I'm longing for the love of heaven,
    Where the weary are at rest.

I'm weary of the friendships broken,
    Of scattered hopes, and severed love,
I'm longing for the true affection,
    In the perfect world above.

I'm longing, Heavenly Father,
    To be safe within the fold,
To see no longer darkly,
    But Thy face in love behold.

Yet I know by past experience,
    That Thou givest what is best ;
Grant then, Lord, faith and patience,
    To await the promised rest.

REMINISCENCES OF A COMMUNION SABBATH,

AT NEWHAVEN FREE CHURCH.

October, 1871.

DARK clouds with gloom enwrapped the sacred morn,
And veiled in the grey canopy of heaven,
The sun his cheering beams of warmth withheld;
Sear withered leaves of autumn strewed the path,
And whirled in the cold blasts that swept the plain,
Presaging winter's hoary presence near.
Like faded hopes that cheered our hearts awhile,
Looking so beauteous, and gladly bright,
No thought had we they e'er would pass away;
But disappointment, like a searing wind,
"Nipt in the bud" our fondly cherished flowers,
And scattered far and wide our short-lived joy.
Thus all on earth fades soon, too soon away,
Nought here can last for ever, we must die,
Though like these leaves we once were fair, and bright,
And proudly rested in our youth and strength,
To shield us safe from all impending ills;
Even death seemed then a thing but seen afar.
But ah! how short the longest life appears,
With nought beyond this tearful vale of earth;
How dark the mystic river we must cross,
When no glad beams of heaven's light, and love,
Gleam o'er the chilling wave to cheer the soul.

In holy peace how blest a christian dies,
When faith's all piercing eye looks through the gloom
Into the bright beyond, where all is love, and light,
Where perfect joy abounds, and peace endures.
And on that hallowed morn of peaceful rest,
Though dark and drear without, our hearts were glad,
For on that day was held the sacred feast,
Commemorative of our Saviour's love
And sacrifice. That holy sacrifice
By which our guilty souls are saved from death,
And well-deserved wrath of God most high.
Oh! love of Christ, how great, how infinite,
Our feeble minds can never understand,
The height, the depth, and all the boundless width
Of that immortal love, which reigned within
The bosom of God's holy Son, that He
Should leave the mansions of the Father's house
To suffer here ; and homeless, have not where
To lay His blessed head. To toil and weep,
And yield His life a ransom for His foes.
But stranger still, if aught more strange may be,
That we, for whom He died, should be so cold
And careless in His cause, and daily show
Such lack of zeal for Him who died to save.
The Lord direct our hearts unto His love,
That we may serve Him, not through fear of wrath,
But for the love wherewith He loved us
When yet we knew of Him, and sought Him not.
We heard the joyful sound of sabbath bells,
And gladly hastened to obey their call ;
And mingling with the throng that now unto

The House of God together took their way,
I met with one whom I for long had known,
Yet knew not until then, that he and I
At the same holy table sat, and in the church
On earth, we members both were of the same;
Methought thus will it be, when in that land
We meet with those whom, when on earth we knew,
Yet knew them not, as pilgrims to the realms
To which ourselves were bound, nor recognised
That bond of brotherhood, the love of Christ,
Which like a golden chain, encircling binds,
More close than earthly ties, the Sons of God.
Along the sea-shore with its changing tides,
We took our way, unto the House of God:
The surging waves, with never-ceasing moan,
Beat wild against their time-worn prison walls,
An emblem meet of those, tossed to and fro
By evil conscience; assuming doctrines dark,
Which they well know to be profanely false,
They with dark zeal inflamed, seek to o'erthrow
Whate'er is good; assailing Zion's walls
With raging waves of arrogance, and hate;
Ne'er thinking that the King, and His dear Son
'Gainst whom they plot, shall surely scorn them all.
In scattered groups upon the shore there stood
The hardy sons of toil, whose dark blue garb,
And easy gait, bespoke their honoured craft;
Honoured by Him, who waiting long ago,
Stood by the rippling sea, at early morn,
And to the weary sons of Zebedee
Spoke kindly words of cheering love and hope,

Crowning their hard but fruitless labour with
A prosperous end. So is He waiting still
To bless and aid us, in our various tasks,
And with His cheering presence, soothe our fears.
The boats that lightly tossed upon the waves
Were anchored fast ; nor could the swelling sea
Nor angry blasts them harm thus safely moored ;
So may our souls, by faith, be fixed on Christ,
The rock of ages. Then though the storms of life
May round us rage, no ills we need to fear,
For winds and waves obey the voice of Him
We trust, in whose hand are the hearts of men.
Into the house of prayer with reverent mien
And willing hearts, they enter ; rich and poor,
A motley throng of old and young they were,
Some glad, some almost gay, but many more
With serious thoughtful look, and tender tone,
That spoke the earnest feelings of their hearts.
And some, who for the first time paid their vows,
And offered unto God their love and youth,
A pleasing sacrifice. And with them those on whom
The hand of time had laid his withering touch,
And marked his lines upon the once smooth brow,
On which, ere long, to write the mystic word
That stamps men for the final stroke of death ;
"As trees are marked for falling," so are they,
"The young may die, the old they must," and soon.
Thrice happy they who in the morn of youth,
Devote to God their strength, and zeal, and love ;
For when the eventide of life draws nigh,
The sun of righteousness shall give them light.

Some there wore sable garments, badge of grief;
The tear scarce dried upon the cheek, the sigh
That breathes the anguish of the heart bereaved;
The vacant seats, where the beloved ones lost
Were wont to sit, bring dark and saddening thoughts,
Of happier days gone bye; and memories stir
In the sad breast, till the dim eyes o'erflow.
Yet why should we thus mourn for friends that were,
As if for ever from our sight they'd gone;
A few short years and then we too must die,
And mingle with the hosts that went before.
What happy meetings then await the just,
Beyond the realms of death, to part no more;
When our High Priest will give us living bread,
And in our cup the new wine richly pour,
Bidding us drink of it, and live for aye.
Then to Kilmarnock's old and plaintive air,
Was sung the solemn psalm, composed by him
Who was the poet-king of Israel.
How sweet those softly tender tunes resound;
They wake the inmost echoes of the heart,
And waft the fancies back to years gone bye,
When in our childhood's homes we heard them sung
By voices that no more are heard below,
But now on high have learned a sweeter strain;
Or backward still, we seem to hear again
The martyr band, in yon wild mountain glen,
Their voices wafted by the evening breeze;
Chanting their noble hymns of faith in God,
To these same simple tunes that now we sing.
Then after prayer, and scripture slowly read,

The text was chosen, and free boundless grace,
Was made the theme ; then with experienced thought
And pleasing speech, the truth divine was shown.
No messenger of wrath was he who spoke,
But offering wisely, mercy full and free,
To these who, through the living way, should seek
To enter into life. Eternal life ; how great,
And how divinely grand, surpassing speech,
And far beyond the limits of our thoughts.
Then came the solemn and impressive work,
Of warning all unworthy guests away,
Who disobeying the dear Lord's command,
Refused the robes of His white righteousness,
When coming to the feast, He had prepared
For every humble soul who fled to Him
Craving His grace for their imperfectness.
But though severe the test to those who came
With out-ward worship, but in heart unclean,
Yet still God's grace was shewn in mercy mild,
Debarring not the sinner, but the sin.
Then after thanks to God, in prayer and praise,
The sacred symbols of the dying Christ
Passed round His table, in remembrance of
His love and last command. Deep silence reigned,
And mid the peaceful hush, the still small voice,
By listening hearts was heard, and many there
Held sweet communion with their risen Lord,
Whose presence consecrates our feast of love.
Then rose our aged Pastor,* well-beloved,
Majestic in his calm simplicity ;

* Dr. Fairbairn.

And in such earnest tones he spoke of faith,
And trust in God, our help and mighty shield,
As wakened kindred feelings in each breast ;
While thoughts of future bliss, and death o'ercome,
Cheered anxious doubting hearts that feared the grave.
With joyful hope, the speaker's eyes grew bright,
And on his brow, a radiance from on high
Fell fair and shining, emblem of the crown
Awaiting him in the glad realms above.
Thus though the day was dark and drear without,
Yet in our fane, shone forth the purest light ;
The sun of righteousness shed beams of love,
Dispelling all our clouds of doubt and fear ;
Nor will these rays grow dim, but brighter shine,
Until we reach that holier happier shore,
Our goal of bliss, where 'mid'st effulgent light,
The house of God, not made with hands appears ;
To which the gathered saints of every creed,
From every clime, will come at last ; to spend
An endless sabbath in the world above.

www.ingramcontent.com/pod-product-compliance
Lightning Source LLC
Chambersburg PA
CBHW030342170426
43202CB00010B/1211